CHAPTER 1

BREAKFASTS

Cinnamon Rolls

Gluten, Tree Nut, Rice and Corn Free.

1. Warm the milk and butter in a small saucepan over medium heat until the mixture reaches about 115 degrees. Transfer the mixture to the bowl of an electric mixer. Then add the yeast and sugar and allow to sit till the yeast is bloomed, about 5 min.

2. Add the egg (slightly beaten), vanilla, salt, guar gum and apple cider vinegar to the mixture. Mix until combined, but not overworking the mixture

3. Combine the cassava flour and arrowroot starch into a bowl and slowly add to the wet mixture and mix on low until all the flour is incorporated.

4. Transfer the dough to a lightly greased bowl, covered with plastic wrap in a warm place and allow to rise for about 1 hour or overnight, in the fridge.

5. Once the dough has risen to just under twice its original size transfer it to a lightly floured surface and roll it until it is about 1/4 in thick rectangle.

6. Rub the butter over the entire surface of the dough. You can add more if you like your cinnamon rolls extra gooey.

7. Combine the sugar, brown sugar and cinnamon into a bowl and then sprinkle the mixture over the buttered dough.

8. Roll the dough into a log and slice into equal sections about 1 inch thick.

9. In a greased baking dish place the cinnamon rolls slightly apart. Pour any remaining filling mixture over the tops of the cinnamon rolls.

10. Let them sit as you preheat the oven to 350 degrees and bake for 15-20 minutes.

11. While the cinnamon rolls bake, in a separate bowl combine the ingredients for the glaze and mix until combined. Allow the cinnamon rolls to cool slightly before applying glaze and enjoy!

Ingredients

1 C Warm Milk
1/3 C Butter
2 1/4 TSP Yeast
1/4 C Sugar
1 TSP Salt
1 TSP Vanilla
1 Egg, Large
1 TSP Guar Gum
1 TSP Apple Cider Vinegar
1 1/2 C Cassava Flour
1 C Arrowroot Starch

Filling:
1/2 C White Sugar
1 C Brown sugar
1 TBS Ground Cinnamon
1/4 C Butter, softened

Glaze:
1/2 C Butter, Soft
1/4 C Cream Cheese
1 1/2 C Powdered Sugar
1 TBS Vanilla
1 TBS Milk

Yield 12 Rolls

Ingredients

2 lbs Pork Butt,
Ground
2 TSP Salt
1/2 TSP Garlic
Powder
1/2 TSP Black
Pepper
1 TBS Sage
1 TBS Thyme
1 TBS Dark Brown
Sugar
1/2 TSP Ground
Fennel Seeds
1/8 TSP Red
Pepper Flakes
1/2 TSP Smoked
Paprika

Breakfast Sausage
Gluten, Tree Nut, Rice, Corn and Dairy Free

1. Combine all the ingredients into a bowl and mix by hand until completely combined.

2. Cover and allow to rest at least 30 minutes.

3. Use in your favorite dish that uses sausage.

Note: This can be made into patties, ground up or added to recipes that require sausage.

You can also freeze and use at a later time.

Yield 2 lbs Sausage

Blueberry Muffins

Gluten, Rice and Corn Free. (Contains Dairy and Coconut)

Ingredients

1 1/3 C Cassava Flour
1/2 C Arrowroot Starch + 1 TBS (Set aside)
1 TBS Coconut Flour
1/2 C Sugar
2 Eggs, Large
1 C Milk of Choice
1/2 TSP Salt
2 TSP Baking Soda
2 TSP Cream of Tartar
1 C Greek Yogurt
1/2 C Avocado Oil
1 TBS Vanilla
1 TSP Lemon Zest
1 C Blueberries

1. Preheat the oven to 350 degrees and line a muffin pan with liners.

2. Combine the cassava flour, arrowroot, coconut flour, salt, baking soda and cream of tartar into a bowl.

3. In a separate bowl cream the eggs, sugar, yogurt and oil until the mixture is light and fluffy.

4. Fold the dry mixture into the wet ingredients until completely combined, but do not over work.

5. Fold the milk, vanilla and lemon zest into the mixture until it is combined.

6. Lightly dust the remaining one TBS of arrowroot starch over the blueberries in a separate bowl. These must be fresh and dried as the excess moisture from frozen berries adds to much moisture to the muffins.

7. Fill a muffin tin lined with liners about 3/4 full. Bake the muffins for 20-25 min until the muffins are slightly golden and a knife inserted into them comes out clean.

Note: This batter works best with fresh not frozen berries.

The batter will expand and slightly fall as they cool. The cassava flour can tend to leave a chewy texture when these are hot but once they completely cool that goes away.

Yield 12 Muffins

Ingredients

1/2 C Butter,
Softened
3/4 C Brown
Sugar
2 Eggs, Large
1 TBS Vanilla
1 TSP Baking Soda
2 TSP Cream of
Tartar
1 TSP Salt
1/2 TSP Cinnamon
1/2 TSP Guar Gum
1 C Cassava Flour
3/4 C Arrowroot
Starch
5 Large Overly
Ripe Bananas

Banana Muffins
Gluten, Tree Nut, Corn and Rice Free. (Contains Diary).

1. Preheat the oven to 375 degrees.

2. Combine the bananas, butter, eggs. vanilla and sugar into the bowl of a stand mixer, or bowl.

3. Mix on medium until the bananas have become mostly mush and the mixture resembles almost a thick syrup. (You might see separation in the ingredients at this point and that is normal.)

4. Add the baking soda, cream of tartar, guar gum, cinnamon and salt to the mixture.

5. Add the cassava flour and the arrowroot to the mixture 1/2 cup at a time until all the flour is mixed into the batter.

6. Line a muffin tin and scoop about 1/4-1/3 cup of batter into the muffin liners. (Should be almost to the top of the liner).

7. Bake for about 20-25 minutes until the muffins have slightly domed and become golden brown in color.

Note: The Cassava flour can leave these a little chewy as they cool. The texture improves as the cool completely.

Yield 12 Muffins

Ingredients

1 1/4 C Milk of Choice
1/2 C Butter, Softened
1/2 TSP Salt
1/4 C Sugar
1 1/3 C Cassava Flour
1/3 C Arrowroot Starch + 1/3 C Set aside
2 TBS Coconut Flour
3 Eggs, Large
1 TBS Yeast
1 TSP Baking Soda
2 TSP Cream of Tartar
Oil for Frying

Glaze:
1/2 C Butter, Softened
1 1/2 C Powdered Sugar
1 TBS Vanilla
1 TBS Milk of Choice

Note: I find if I want the traditional donut shape freezing works best. When I am just whipping up our daughters favorite donut holes I will pipe them directly into the oil.

Watch your oil temperature as this dough does take a little bit to cook all the way through and if the oil is to hot it will not cook evenly throughout the donut.

Donuts

Gluten, Rice and Corn Free. (Contains Coconut)

1. In a pan over medium heat, combine the milk and butter until completely melted and warmed until about 110 degrees.

2. To the pan add the sugar and stir till combined.

3. Remove the pan from the heat and whisk in the eggs one at a time. Add the yeast once it has cooled a little from the sugar.

4. Then add in the salt, baking soda and cream of tartar and mix into the mixture.

5. Fold in the cassava flour, arrowroot starch and coconut flour until a soft dough forms.

6. Transfer the dough to a bowl, cover with a warm towel and allow to rise for at least an hour. The dough will rise about twice the original size when done.

7. Once the dough has risen carefully fold in the additional arrowroot starch.

8. The dough will be soft. You can either pipe out donut shapes onto a sheet pan covered in parchment paper and freeze before frying to a golden brown or you can transfer the dough into a piping bag and pipe desired shapes directly into the oil when you are ready to cook them.

9. Bring a shallow pot of oil to medium-low heat. Drop the desired donut shapes into the oil and let them cool until they are golden brown on all sides.

10. While the donuts slightly cool, in a separate bowl combine the glaze ingredients until combined. Lightly coat the donuts into the glaze and enjoy!

Yield 2-3 Dozen Donuts

Pancakes

Gluten, Tree Nut, Rice and Corn Free. (Diary Free Options,)

Ingredients

1 C Cassava Flour
1/3 C Arrowroot Starch
1 TBS Psyllium Husk Powder
1/4 C Sugar
1/2 C Butter or Ghee, Softened
1/2 TSP Baking Soda
1 TSP Cream of Tartar
1 TBS Vanilla
1/2 Lemon Squeezed or 1 TBS Lemon Juice
3 Eggs, Large
1/2 TSP Salt
1 1/2 C Milk of Choice
1/2 C Blueberries or other favorite add-ins.

1. Mix cassava flour, arrowroot starch, psyllium husk powder, sugar, butter (or Ghee), baking soda and cream of tartar into a bowl until the mixture becomes crumbly. Do not overly mix it you want to see small clumps of butter in the mixture still.

2. Next add in the vanilla, lemon juice and eggs and whisk until combined.

3. Then add the milk and whisk until combined. At this point you can add any additions if you desire. Our girls love blueberries, strawberries and sometimes chocolate chips. (Make sure to use fresh berries that have been dried after washing to reduce extra moisture into the batter)

4. Allow the mixture to sit about 5 minutes. In the meantime heat a griddle to medium heat and slightly grease with desired method.

5. Once griddle is warm place 1/4 cup of the mixture on the griddle. I like to slightly shake the griddle side to side to let the mixture settle evenly. Allow too cook until bubbles form throughout the pancake and then flip. It should take about 2 minutes per side.

6. Top with butter, maple syrup or other desired toppings and enjoy.

Yield 8, 4 inch Pancakes

Note: Make sure berries are not frozen if added.

Waffles

Gluten, Tree Nut, Rice and Corn Free. (Diary Free Options,)

Ingredients

1 C Cassava Flour
1/3 C Arrowroot Starch
1 TBS Psyllium Husk Powder
1 TBS Vanilla
3 Eggs, Large
1/2 C Butter or Ghee, Softened
1/2 TSP Baking Soda
1 TSP Cream of Tartar
1/4 C Sugar
1/2 TSP Salt
1 1/2 C Milk of Choice
2 TBS Avocado Oil
1/2 C Blueberries or other favorite add-ins, Optional

1. Combine the cassava flour, arrowroot, psyllium husk powder, baking soda, cream of tartar, sugar and butter into a bowl until it is crumbly. Do not overly mix it you want to see small clumps of butter in the mixture still.

2. Next add the vanilla and eggs then whisk until the eggs are mixed evenly into the batter.

3. Then add the milk and oil and mix just until combined.

You can also stir in any add-ins at this time. Make sure any additional ingredients are fresh and dry to ensure extra moisture does not enter the batter.

4. Allow the mixture to sit about 5 minutes while you preheat a waffle iron to be about medium heat.

5. Cook the batter in a preheated waffle iron until slightly golden brown on both sides. Make sure that your iron does not get overly hot as this will make the waffles cook unevenly.

6. Top with some additional butter, ghee, syrup or favorite topping of your own and enjoy!

Note: Make sure berries are not frozen if added.

Yield 8, 4 in Waffles

Ingredients

9 Eggs, Large
1 C Milk of Choice
1/2 C Cassava Flour
1/4 C Arrowroot Starch
6 TBS Butter or Ghee
1 TSP Vanilla
1/4 TSP Salt
1/4 TSP Baking Soda
1/2 TSP Cream of Tartar

German Pancakes
Gluten, Tree Nut, Rice and Corn Free. (Diary Free Options).

1. Preheat oven to 450 degrees. While the oven is preheating place a cast iron pan, or regular baking (8x8 or 9x13) dish of choice into the oven to allow the dish to preheat as the oven does. Once the oven is at 450 degrees add the butter to the pan and allow it to melt, making sure to move the pan and allow the butter to coat the bottom of the pan.

2. In a bowl, beat the eggs, milk and vanilla until they are fluffy.

3. In a separate bowl mix the remaining dry ingredients.

4. Slowly mix the dry ingredients into the egg mixture until it is completely incorporated. I like to fold the mixture in to allow as much of the eggs to remain as fluffy as possible.

5. Once the oven and pan have been completely preheated to the 450 degrees and the butter or ghee is melted then slowly pour the mixture into the hot pan.

6. Bake for about 15-18 minutes until the mixture begins to rise and slightly brown on the top.

7. Remove the pan from the oven, Slice and top with your favorite topping and maybe some powdered sugar.

Note: While the mixture does rise in the oven sometimes it can sink depending on the type of pan used, this is normal.

This pairs great with my Sweet Berry Sauce on page 24.

Serves 4-6 People

Sweet Berry Syrup

Gluten, Tree Nut, Rice, Corn and Diary Free.

Ingredients

2 C Berries of Choice, Fresh or Frozen
1/2 Maple Syrup
1/2- 1 C Orange Juice
1/2 TBS Vanilla
1/4 TSP Salt
1 TSP Ground Cinnamon

1. Combine all ingredients into a medium sized saucepan over medium-high heat.

2. Stir on occasion until the sugar has dissolved and the mixture has started to slightly boil.

3. Reduce the heat to low and simmer for about 10-15 minutes until the berries have softened and started to blister and fall apart.

4. If there are any large berry pieces left in the sauce either take a potato masher or fork and smash them into the sauce until the pieces of fruit are about all equal. If you want a smoother sauce you can put it in the blender and pulse it until smooth.

5. Allow sauce to cool for about 5 minutes and serve.

Note: This is a sweet treat to top onto pancakes, waffles, crepes and even ice cream to add some berry goodness. Our daughters love this sauce. I will change up the berries depending what is in season or whatever they are feeling then. It is always a hit!

Yield 1 1/2 C Syrup

Sweet Potato Breakfast Hash

Gluten, Tree Nut, Rice and Corn Free. (Diary Free Options)

Ingredients

2 Sweet Potatoes
6 Strips of Bacon, or 1 lb Sausage
1/2 Yellow Onion
1/2 Yellow Bell Pepper
1/2 Red Bell Pepper
1/2 Green Bell Pepper
1 C Mushrooms
2 TBS Butter or Ghee
1 TBS Garlic
1 TSP Salt
1 TBS Smoked Paprika

Optional to Top: Eggs Cooked to liking, Avocado, Cheese, Salsa

1. Preheat the oven to 425 degrees.

2. On a sheet pan lined with a metal rack lay the bacon on top of the metal rack on the pan. Bake the bacon for about 20 min until it starts to get crispy. Remove the bacon from the oven and set aside. If using sausage, cook it in a pan on medium heat until it is cooked through and starting to brown a bit.

3. While the bacon or sausage cooks, dice the sweet potatoes (peeled or un-peeled depending on preference) and place in a pan over medium heat with the ghee. If using sausage just add the potatoes to the pan with the sausage once it has started to cook.

4. Once the sweet potatoes have started to caramelize dice and add the bell peppers, onion and mushrooms to the pan. I like to make them about the size of the diced sweet potatoes.

5. Let them cook until all the vegetables have started to cook through and caramelize a bit, about 10 minutes.

6. If using bacon, once it is cooked, rough chop it and add it the pan with the sweet potatoes and vegetables.

7. Add the spices and additional ghee if desired.

8. In a separate pan cook eggs in quantity and likeness.

9. Once everything is cooked place the sweet potato hash into a bowl, top it with eggs of choice, cheese, avocado and salsa or other desired toppings and enjoy!

Serves 4-6 People

Bagels

Gluten, Tree Nut, Rice and Corn Free. Diary Free Options.

Ingredients

1 1/2 C Cassava Flour
1 1/2 C Arrowroot Starch
1 3/4 C Milk or Water
2 TBS Yeast
2 TSP Guar Gum
1/2 TSP Salt
2 TBS Avocado Oil
1 TBS Sugar
1 TBS Apple Cider Vinegar

Optional Additions:
1 C Fresh Blueberries
1 TBS Cinnamon
1 C Cheese

1. Heat milk or water till it reaches about 110 degrees, add the yeast and allow to rest for about 5 min until it has bloomed.

2. In a separate bowl mix the cassava flour, arrowroot, guar gum, salt and sugar. Stir to combine.

3. Add the liquid and yeast mixture to the dry ingredients and fold until combined.

4. Add the oil and apple cider vinegar and fold to combine.

5. At this point you can add in flavor options if desired. A cup of fresh blueberries or even cinnamon and raisins. Our daughters love blueberry bagels.

6. Divide the dough into 12 balls and place onto a sheet pan lined with parchment paper.

7. With wet hands form the bagel shape by smoothing out the balls and making a hole in the center with your finger. Place back on the parchment paper.

8. Brush the tops of the bagels lightly with oil, cover with plastic wrap and allow to rise for about 30-45 min. They will rise but do not let them reach more than double their size.

9. When the bagels are finished rising, bring a pot of water to a rolling boil and preheat the oven to 450 degrees.

10. One at a time place the bagels into the boiling water and allow them to boil until they start to float. This should take about 30 seconds to 1 minutes on each side.

11. Once they have boiled place them back onto the parchment lined sheet pan.

12. At this point you can either top the bagels with cheese, a favorite spice mixture (Everything bagel from Trader Joe's is a hit) or leave them plain.

13. Bake the bagels for about 20-25 min until the bagels are slightly golden brown.

Yield 12 Bagels

Note: The Cassava can leave these a little chewy while cooling. The texture improves as they cool and better when toasted once cooled.

CHAPTER 2

PASTA

Cassava Flour Pasta

Gluten, Tree Nut, Rice, Corn and Diary Free

Ingredients

1 1/4 C Cassava Flour
1/2 C Tapioca Starch
5 Eggs, Large
1 TBS Olive or
Avocado Oil
1 TSP Salt
1/2 TSP Garlic
Powder

1. In a stand mixer with the paddle attachment place the eggs, oil and spices and until combined.

2. Add the tapioca starch to the egg mixture, and combine.

3. Add the cassava flour in 1/4 cup increments, mixing on low between each 1/4 cup.

4. The dough will start to form a playdough texture ball when it is ready. You might not need all of the cassava flour for this to happen. It depends on the size of your eggs and the moisture volumes.

5. Once the dough has been formed and has a playdough texture, place it on a lightly floured piece of parchment paper and knead the dough until it is smooth.

6. Roll the dough into desired shapes using either a rolling pin or a pasta press.

To Cook:

1. Bring a pot of water to a slight boil and add a 1/4 TSP of salt.

2. Add the pasta and boil for about 5-7 minutes until it starts to float a little and becomes tender. Time may vary depending on how thick the pasta is or desired shape.

3. Top with your favorite sauce and enjoy!

Note: This pasta does expand as it is cooked to about double the thickness. I find making sure the pasta is thinner than I want it to be before cooking yields a better result.

Serves 4-6

Ingredients

1/2 lb Bacon
1 lb Boneless, Skinless, Chicken Breasts
2 TBS Olive Oil
1/2 Yellow Onion
1 C Portabella Mushrooms
1 8 oz Can of Diced Tomatoes
1/2 C Chicken Stock
1 8 oz Block of Cream Cheese
1/2 C Parmesan or Romano Cheese
1 TSP Salt
2 TBS Garlic
1 TBS Parsley
2 TBS Italian Seasoning.

Chicken Carbonara Sauce
Gluten, Tree Nut, Rice and Corn Free.

1. Dice the raw bacon into small cubes and place into a pan and allow it to cook until it is fully cooked and on the crunchy side, set aside.

2. Drain half the bacon grease from the pan and add the olive oil to the pan. Thinly slice the chicken and add it to the pan and allow it to cook thoroughly.

3. Slice the onion and mushrooms and add them to the pan with the chicken until they start to caramelize.

4. Next add the diced tomatoes (undrained) and the chicken stock and allow it to come to a simmer.

5. When the mixture starts to simmer add the cream cheese and stir until it is completely melted.

6. Once the cream cheese is melted, stir in the spices, the reserved bacon and the choice of either Parmesan or Romano cheese and let it simmer until the sauce thickens.

7, Serve with a batch of my Cassava Flour Pasta on pg 32 or over your favorite gluten free pasta or even spaghetti squash and enjoy!

Serves 4-6

Alfredo Sauce

Gluten, Tree Nut, Rice and Corn Free

Ingredients

1/2 C Butter
8 oz Cream Cheese
2 C Heavy Whipping Cream
2 Garlic Cloves, chopped or 1 TBS Ground
1 TSP Salt
1 TBS Italian Seasoning
1/2 C Grated Parmesan Cheese
1/2 C Grated Romano Cheese
1/4 C Asiago Cheese
2 TBS Fresh Parsley to top.

Optional:
Chicken, Mushrooms, Broccoli

1. In a skillet melt the butter and cream cheese over medium heat until combined, stirring occasionally.

2. Add the heavy whipping cream and cook over medium heat until the sauce starts to thicken.

3. Add the cheeses and spices and simmer about 5-10 min until desired thickness is achieved.

4. You can add grilled chicken, sautéed mushrooms or broccoli for additional taste and textures as desired.

5. Serve with a fresh batch of my Cassava Flour Pasta on pg 32 or with your favorite gluten free pasta and enjoy.

Serves 4-6

Yakisoba

Gluten, Rice, Corn and Dairy Free. (Nut Free Options).

1. Prepare the noodles by boiling them. Once they are boiled, add 2 TBS avocado oil into a large skillet and lightly fry the noodles until they get a little golden in their color and then set them aside

2. In that same pan add the remaining avocado oil and sliced chicken into the skillet and cook until the chicken is cooked through, about 5-10 minutes.

3. Once the chicken is cooked add the onions, carrots, broccoli, bell peppers and mushrooms. Stirring occasionally cook until fork tender, 5-10 minutes.

4. Mix all of the sauce ingredients into a small bowl and whisk until combined, set aside.

5. Add the cabbage to the meat and vegetable mixture and stir until the cabbage has started to wilt, about 5 minutes.

6. Add the sauce to the mixture and bring to a slight simmer until the sauce starts to thicken, 5-10 minutes.

7. Add in the noodles and sliced green onions and stir until the noodles are coated and enjoy!

Ingredients

1 Batch GF Noodles of choice
1 lb Chicken Breasts thinly sliced or meat of choice (Can use pork and/or seafood.)
1/2 Yellow Onion, thinly sliced
2 Carrots, cut into ribbons
2 Green Onions, Sliced
1/2 Medium, Greed Cabbage, Thinly Sliced
1 C Shiitake Mushrooms, Sliced
1 C Broccoli, Chopped
1 Red Bell Pepper, Thinly Sliced
4 TBS Avocado Oil, divided

For the Sauce:
1/4 C Dark Brown Sugar
1/4 C Coconut Aminos or GF Soy Sauce
4 TBS Tomato Paste
1 TBS Apple Cider Vinegar
1/2 TSP Ginger, Minced
2 Garlic Cloves, Minced
1/2 TSP Salt
1 TBS Tapioca Starch

Serves 4-6

Ingredients

4 TBS Butter or
Ghee
4 OZ Cream
Cheese
1 C Milk or Heavy
Whipping Cream
2 Cloves of Garlic,
minced or 1 TBS
Garlic Powder
1/4 TSP Salt
Zest of 1 Lemon
1/4 C Fresh Lemon
Juice, about two
lemons worth
1/2 C White Wine
or Chicken Stock
2 TBS Fresh Parsley

Optional:
1/4 C Parmesan
Cheese

Creamy Lemon Garlic Sauce
Gluten, Tree Nut, Rice and Corn Free. (Contains Dairy).

1. In a skillet over medium heat add the butter or ghee and allow it to cook until almost melted.

2. Add the garlic and allow it to cook until slightly browned. This will bring out the sweet and slightly nutty flavor in the garlic.

3. Turn the heat to low and add the lemon zest, lemon juice and white wine or chicken stock. Allow the mixture to simmer for about 5-10 minutes

4. Add the cream cheese and milk or cream and mix until combined.

5. Toss over a batch of fresh Cassava Flour Pasta on pg 32 or even some roasted spaghetti squash. Top with additional lemon zest and some Parmesan cheese if you like it.

Yield 3 Cups

Creamy Roasted Red Pepper Sauce

Gluten, Tree Nut, Rice, and Corn Free. (Contains Dairy).

1. Dice the onion, artichokes, roasted red peppers and mushrooms in half the butter until softened and slightly browned.

2. Add the chicken stock, remaining butter and heavy cream, simmer until it starts to thicken.

3. Add spices and cheese and simmer the sauce until desired thickness is achieved.

4. Serve over my Cassava Flour Noodles on pg 32 or some fresh zoodles and enjoy!

Ingredients

1/2 Yellow Onion
1 14 oz Can of Non Marinated Artichokes
1 Jar Roasted Red Peppers (Or roast your own)
1 C Crimini Mushrooms
4 TBS Butter, or Ghee, Split
2 C Chicken Stock
1 C Heavy Cream
1/4 C Romano Cheese
4 Gloves of Garlic
1 TBS Herbs De Province Seasoning
1/2 TSP Crushed Red Pepper Flakes
1/2 TSP Salt

Yield 3 Cups

Potato Gnocchi

Gluten, Tree Nut, Rice, Corn Free. Diary Free Options.

Ingredients

3-4 M Potatoes
1/2 C Cassava Flour
1/4 C Tapioca Starch
1 Egg, Large
1 TBS Butter or Ghee
1/2 TSP Salt

1. Bake the potatoes at 375 degrees until fork tender about 30-45 min. (I like to put mine in a covered Dutch oven to help maintain moisture and not overly bake the potatoes.)

2. Once the potatoes are cooked, peel them while they are still warm. (The skins will come off easier.) Place the peeled potatoes into the bowl of a stand mixer and add the remaining ingredients.

3. Mix on a medium speed until the mixture forms a dough and starts to ball up and pull away from the edges.

4. Allow the mixture to cool a few minutes.

5. Once the dough has cooled some. roll the dough into a ball. Cut the dough into smaller pieces to work with and roll them until you have a rope of dough that is about a half an inch wide.

6. Cut the rope into 1/2 inch chunks. Roll each piece down the back side of a fork. This helps to seal the pieces and give them their traditional shape. Alternatively you an simply use your thumb and press the pieces into shape or make any other shape you prefer.

7. At this point you can freeze them for later use or cook them.

To Cook:
1. Bring a pot of water to a boil and add 1/2 TSP Salt.

2. Boil the gnocchi for about 3-5 min or until they begin to float.

3. Set aside until all are boiled.

4. To give the more pasta like texture to the gnocchi. Slightly fry them in a saucepan with a little bit of butter or ghee.

5. Top with your favorite sauce or use in your favorite dishes, and enjoy!

Serves 4-6

Ingredients

1 Batch Potato
Gnocchi
1/2 C Butter, or
ghee
1/3 C Tapioca
Starch
3 C Milk of Choice
2 TSP Garlic
Powder
1 TSP Salt
11/4 TSP Thyme
1/8 TSP Rosemary
1/4 TSP Paprika
2 1/2 C Shredded
Cheese (Cheddar
or a mixture if you
prefer)

Gnocchi Mac and Cheese
Gluten, Tree Nut, Rice and Corn Free. (Contains Dairy).

1. Take one batch of potato gnocchi, boil and allow them to slightly crisp in a pan and then set aside.

2 Preheat the oven to 350 degrees.

3. In a saucepan over medium heat, melt the butter, or ghee and add the tapioca starch until a paste forms.

4. Add the milk of choice and spices and cook over medium heat until it starts to thicken.

5. Once the sauce has thickened, add the cheese, reserving half a cup for later and continue to stir and cook until the cheese is completely melted. The sauce will continue to thicken.

6. Put the cooked gnocchi into the cheese sauce and stir until combined.

7. Transfer the gnocchi and sauce into an oven proof pan, or casserole dish.

8. Top the mac and cheese with the remaining cheese that was set aside. Bake the mac and cheese for about 30-45 minutes until the cheese completely melted and the top starts to brown.

9. Allow to cool 5-10 min once done, and enjoy!

Serves 4-6

Ingredients

1 Batch GF Pasta
1-2 lbs Sirloin Steak, Thinly Sliced
1 Yellow Onion
3 Cloves of garlic, crushed or 2 TBS powdered
2 C Mushrooms, Sliced
3 TBS Tapioca Starch
2 TBS Balsamic Vinegar
1/2 TSP Salt
1 1/2 TSP Pepper
2 TBS Olive Oil
1 TBS Butter or Ghee
2 C Beef Stock, or Broth
1/2 C Sour Cream, or dairy free milk of choice.
1 TBS Lemon Juice
1-2 TBS Fresh Parsley

Beef Stroganoff

Gluten, Tree Nut, Rice, and Corn Free. (Dairy Free Options).

1. Make the cassava pasta and put into desired shape. For this dish I tend to make mine into little rectangles and then twist before boiling. Set pasta aside.

2. In a skillet over medium-high heat add the olive oil, sliced onions, mushrooms and garlic then cook until the onions start to wilt and become translucent.

3. Add the strips of sirloin, salt, and pepper. Stir until the steak starts to cook to about medium, some pink will still showing. This should take about 5-10 min depending on how much steak you have.

4. Once the steak reaches to about medium add the butter or ghee along with the tapioca starch. Stir until all the meat is coated and no clumps of the flour remains.

5. Add the beef stock, bring it to a boil and then simmer until the sauce thickens to desired consistency.

6. Turn off the heat, stir in the sour cream or dairy free milk of choice and the lemon juice until combined.

7. Top with fresh parsley and enjoy!

Serves 4-6

Lasagna

Gluten, Tree Nut, Rice and Corn Free. (Contains Dairy).

1. Preheat your oven to 375 degrees.

Prepare the Pasta:
1. Make the pasta. Roll the pasta to about 1/16 to 1/8 In thick. Cut into long, wide strips. I like to make mine about 1/3 the width of my pan by the length of them so each layer gets three equal pieces. *Do not boil the pasta.*

Make the Sauces:
1. In a sauce pan cook the ground beef or turkey and onion until the meat is fully cooked and the onion has become translucent.

2. Add half of the spices, the pasta sauce and the tomato paste to the meat and allow it to simmer, and then set it aside to slightly cool.

3. In a medium bowl add the ricotta cheese, egg, the remaining spices and half the cheese, then mix until combined and set aside.

Assemble:
1. Place a small layer of the meat sauce into the bottom of the pan and then place a layer of the pasta noodles over that.

2. In an alternating fashion lay the ricotta cheese sauce, pasta and meat layers until your pan is full. I tend to have about 6 layers worth in my 9x13 pan since it is a little deeper than most baking dishes..

3. For the top add any additional meat sauce on and then cover the top with remaining cheeses.

4. Bake for about 45-1 hr until the sauce has started to bubble and the cheese on top has started to brown a little bit.

5. Allow to cook about 10 min, slice and enjoy!

Serves 4-6

Ingredients

1-2 Batches of Cassava Pasta
1-2 lbs Ground Beef, or Turkey or combo
1 Medium, Yellow Onion, small diced
3 Cloves of Garlic, or 2 TBS ground
4 C of Favorite Pasta Sauce
1/4 C Tomato Paste
2 TSP Basil
1 1/2 TSP Salt
1 TSP Oregano
1 TSP Thyme
2 TBS Parsley
16 OZ Ricotta Cheese
1 Egg, Large
3 C Mozzarella Cheese
2 C Romano Cheese
1 C Parmesan Cheese

Note: Depending on the size of your baking dish, you may need more than one batch of pasta.

Ingredients

1 batch GF Pasta

Filling:
1 16 OZ Ricotta
Cheese
1/2 C Parmesan
Cheese
1/2 C Romano
Cheese
1 TBS Olive Oil
1 TSP Salt
1 TBS Garlic
Powder
1/2 TSP Parsley
1/2 TSP Marjoram
1/4 TSP Basil
1/8 TSP Lavender,
dried
2 Eggs, separated
1 TBS Water

Tools: I like to use
a ravioli maker to
help get uniform
pieces but you can
completely cut
these by hand as
well.

Cheesy Ravioli
Gluten, Tree Nut, Rice, and Corn Free. (Contains Dairy).

.

.

Make the Filling:
1. In a bowl combine the cheeses, olive oil, spices and one egg
and then mix until it is combined, set aside.

Assemble:
1. Roll out the cassava flour pasta to about 1/16th of an inch or
thinner. I like to use a ravioli maker so I will cut my piece large
enough to cover the form. You can completely do these by
hand by either cutting each square by hand or making a large
rectangle to cut into squares later.

2. Once you have your first layer of pasta in place in desired
shape; spoon about a 3/4 TBS into the center areas of your
prepared pasta. If doing a large rectangle make rows of the
filling while leaving space between to seal the top layer of
pasta and subsequently cut later.

3. Make an egg wash with the remaining egg and water in a
small bowl. Brush the edges around each ravioli with the egg
wash.

4. Roll another layer of the pasta the same as the first. Cover
the ravioli, making sure not to disturb the small mounds of
filling.

5. Cut each ravioli out and secure the edges of each piece by
using the back of a fork to pinch the edges or use a ravioli
cutter and set aside.

To Cook:
1. Bring a saucepan of water to a low boil.

2. Boil the ravioli in batches about 5-7 minutes until they start
to float around and the pasta looks cooked.

3. Cover with your favorite sauce and enjoy!

Serves 4-6

CHAPTER 3

MAIN DISHES

Ingredients

For the Sauce:
1/2 C Honey
1/8 C Sriracha
4 Garlic Cloves,
Minced or 3 TBS
Ground + 1 TSP
Ground, Separated
2 TBS Apple Cider
Vinegar
2 TBS Coconut
Aminos or GF Soy
Sauce
1/2 TSP Salt
1 1/2 TBS Fresh
Lime Juice
2 TBS Avocado Oil,
divided
2 LBS Chicken
Pieces of Choice

Optional:
Sesame Seeds

Honey Sriracha Chicken
Gluten, Dairy, Rice and Corn Free. (Nut Free Options).

1. In a small sauce pan over medium heat, combine everything except the chicken and sesame seeds.

2. Allow mixture to simmer about 5 minutes then set it aside to cool slightly.

3. Preheat the oven to 400 degrees.

4. In a shallow baking dish arrange your chicken of choice. Brush the chicken with the set aside avocado oil and then sprinkle the set aside garlic powder, rotating to coat all sides of the chicken.

5. Pour half of the sauce onto the chicken and rotate to coat.

6. Bake the chicken for about 30-45 minutes, rotating chicken pieces halfway, until chicken is cooked through.

7. Brush with additional sauce if desired.

8. Put the oven on broil and broil the chicken, rotating to finish letting the sauce to caramelize on the chicken and the skin to crisp a little more.

9. Brush with remaining sauce and top with sesame seeds if desired and enjoy!

Serves 4-6

Ingredients

2 lbs Chicken, Cuts
of Choice
1/8 C Avocado Oil
1 C Pineapple Juice
1/2 Brown Sugar
1/4 C Tomato Paste
3 TBS Apple Cider
Vinegar
2 TBS Coconut
Aminos or GF Soy
Sauce
1 TSP Dry Mustard
1 TBS Sriracha
Sauce
1 TSP Garlic
Powder
1 TSP Salt
1/2 TSP Ginger,
Ground
1/2 TSP Onion
Powder
1/8 C Tapioca
Starch

Hawaiian Glazed Chicken
Gluten, Diary, Rice and Corn Free. (Nut Free Options).

1. In a bowl or Ziploc bag add the chicken and avocado oil to coat, set aside.

2. Mix the remaining ingredients together, minus the tapioca starch into a small bowl and whisk to combine.

3. Pour half the sauce into the bowl with the chicken, let sit at least 30 minutes but no more than 4 hours as the pineapple juice can break down the chicken. Reserve the other half of the sauce.

4. When ready to cook the chicken preheat the oven to 400 degrees.

5. Line the chicken into the a shallow baking dish. Bake the chicken for about 30-45 minutes until the chicken is cooked through.

6. While the chicken is cooking combine the remaining sauce and the tapioca starch into a small saucepan over medium heat. Allow the sauce to simmer until it has thickened to desired consistency.

7. Once the chicken has cooked through, brush the tops of the chicken with additional sauce as desired and enjoy!

Serves 4-6

Moroccan Chicken

Gluten, Tree Nut, Rice and Corn Free. (Dairy Free Options).

1. Preheat the oven to 325 degrees.

2. In a heavy bottom dutch over medium heat add the butter and chicken to sear it slightly on all sides, pull chicken out and set aside.

3. Add additional oil if needed and onions and cook until the onions have started to turn translucent but not quite caramelized yet.

4. While the onions are cooking combine the remaining ingredients into a food processor or blender and process until a smooth sauce has formed.

5. Return the chicken to the dutch oven on the stove and add the sauce.

6. Transfer the dutch oven to the oven and cook for 1-3 hours until chicken is fork tender.

7. Serve with your favorite potatoes or try along side my Turmeric Cauliflower "Rice" on pg 82

Ingredients

2 lbs Boneless, Skinless Chicken Breasts
1/4 Tomato Paste
3 C Chicken Stock
1 C Tomato Puree
1/2 TSP Cinnamon
1/4 TSP Cumin
4 Dates
3 Cloves or Garlic, or
1 1/2 TSP Ground
1/4 TSP Coriander
1/4 TSP Parsley
1 Yellow Onion, Diced
11 1/2 Mint Leaves, Fresh
2 TBS Olive Oil
1 TSP Salt
2 TBS Butter or Ghee

Serves 4-6

Sesame Chicken

Gluten, Dairy, Rice and Corn Free. (Contains Coconut).

For the Chicken:
1. Combine the chicken and eggs into a bowl and let sit.

2. Place the flours and spices into a separate bowl.

3. In a shallow skillet fill it with the frying oil and bring to a medium-high point to allow the chicken to fry.

4. While the oil is heating up transfer the chicken from the egg mixture to the flour mixture to coat.

5. Working in batches fry the pieces of chicken in the oil and set aside once done to drain the excess oil off of the chicken while you cook the remaining pieces.

For the Sauce:
1. Combine the sauce ingredients into a small saucepan over medium heat and whisk until combined. Allow the sauce to simmer about 10 minutes until the sauce has thickened.

To Eat:
Toss the Chicken into the sauce once it has thickened, top with sesame seeds if desired and enjoy!

This pairs well with my Asian Roasted Broccoli and Carrots on pg 103.

Ingredients

For the Chicken:
1 lb Chicken Breasts, cut into 1 inch pieces
Oil for Frying
2 Eggs, Large and Slightly Beaten
1/2 C Coconut Flour
1/4 C Tapioca Starch
1/2 TSP Garlic Powder
1/4 TSP Salt

For the Sauce:
1/8 C Sesame Oil
2 Cloves Garlic, Minced
1/4 C Apple Cider Vinegar
1/8 C Honey
2 TBS Sriracha Sauce
4 TBS Tomato Paste
3 TBS Dark Brown Sugar
1/8 C Coconut Aminos or GF Soy Sauce
1 TBS Tapioca Starch

Optional:
2 TBS Sesame Seeds

Serves 4-6

Ingredients

For the Chicken:
1 lb Chicken Breasts, cut
into 1 inch pieces
2 Eggs,Large and Slightly
beaten
1/2 C Coconut Flour
1/4 C Tapioca Starch
1/2 TSP Salt
1/2 TSP Garlic
1/2 TSP Ginger
1/4 TSP Chinese 5 Spice
Oil for Frying

For the Sauce:
1/4 C Coconut Aminos
2 TBS Apple Cider
Vinegar
2 TBS Chicken Broth
1 TBS Sesame Seed Oil
1 TBS Tapioca Starch
2 Cloves of Garlic, or 2
TSP ground
1 in piece of ginger or 2
TSP ground
1/4 C Brown Sugar or
Molasses
2 TBS Tomato Paste
8 Dried Red Chinese or
Arbol Chillies
1/2 C Green Onions

Optional:
Sesame Seeds

General Tso's Chicken
Gluten, Rice and Corn Free. Diary Free Options. (Contains Coconut).

For the Chicken:
1. Combine the chicken and eggs into a bowl and let sit.

2. Place the flours and spices into a separate bowl.

3. In a shallow skillet fill it with the frying oil and bring to a medium-high point to allow the chicken to fry.

4. While the oil is heating up transfer the chicken from the eggs to the flour mixture to coat.

5. Working in batches fry the pieces of chicken in the oil and set aside once done to drain the excess oil off of the chicken while you cook the remaining pieces.

For the Sauce:
1. Combine the sauce ingredients into a small saucepan over medium heat and whisk until combined. Allow the sauce to simmer about 10 minutes until the sauce has thickened.

To Eat:
1. Toss the Chicken into the sauce once it has thickened, top with green onions or sesame seeds if desired and enjoy!

Serves 4-6

Ingredients

For the Chicken:
1 lb Chicken Breasts
1/2 C Coconut Flour
1/4 C Tapioca Starch
Oil for Frying

For the Sauce:
1 C Red Bell Pepper,
Chopped
1 C Green Bell Pepper,
Chopped
1/2 Yellow Onion,
Chopped
1 C Pineapple Chunks
2 TBS Avocado Oil
1 C Pineapple Juice
1/4 C Tomato Paste
2 TBS Apple Cider
Vinegar
1/8 C Light Brown
Sugar
1 TSP Salt
1 TSP Garlic Powder
1/8 C Tapioca Starch

Sweet and Sour Chicken

Gluten, Rice and Corn Free. Diary Free Options. (Contains Coconut).

For the Chicken:
1. Combine the chicken and eggs into a bowl and let sit.

2. Place the flours and spices into a separate bowl.

3. In a shallow skillet fill it with the frying oil and bring to a medium-high point to allow the chicken to fry.

4. While the oil is heating up transfer the chicken from the eggs to the four mixture to coat.

5. Working in batches fry the pieces of chicken in the oil and set aside once done to drain the excess oil off of the chicken while you cook the remaining pieces.

For the Sauce:
1. Combine the remaining sauce ingredients into a small saucepan over medium heat and whisk until combined. Allow to simmer about 10 minutes until the sauce has thickened.

To Eat:
1. Toss the Chicken into the sauce once it has thickened, This pairs well with my Cauliflower Fried "Rice" on pg 84

Serves 4-6

Crispy Lemon Pork Scallopini

Gluten, Rice and Dairy Free.(Contains Coconut).

Ingredients

1 lb thin cut pork chops, or thick cut, cut in half
1/2 C Lemon Juice, Fresh
1/4 C Avocado Oil + 2 TBS Set Aside
3 Cloves Garlic, or 1 1/2 TSP Ground + 1/4 TSP Ground Set Aside
1/2 TSP Pink Salt + 1/4 TSP Set Aside
1 TBS Italian Seasoning + 1 TSP Set Aside
1/2 C Coconut Flour
1/4 C Tapioca Starch

1. Cut the pork chops in half, thickness wise if needed. Place the pork chops between two pieces of parchment paper and using a meat mallet prepare the chicken until it is about an 1/8 of an inch in thickness.

2. In a shallow dish combine the lemon juice and spices

3. Add the pork chops and allow to sit for about 30 minutes to an hour.

4. In a skillet heat the reserved avocado oil over medium heat.

5. Combine the flours and reserved spices in a shallow dish.

6. Dredge the pieces of pork chop from the lemon juice mixture into the flour mixture and then place in the warmed skillet. Allow to cook until the outside becomes crisp about 3-5 minutes per side.

7. Allow to cool slightly and enjoy!

Serves 4-6

Crispy Fried Chicken
Gluten, Tree Nut, Rice, and Corn Free (Dairy Free Options).

Ingredients

2-4 lbs Chicken, in desired pieces.
4 C Milk of Choice
1 TBS Garlic Powder
1 1/2 TSP Salt + 1/2 TSP Set Aside
1 TSP Paprika
1 TSP Onion Powder
1/8 TSP Thyme
1/4 TSP Mustard Powder
1/4 TSP Sage
1/8 TSP Cinnamon
1 C Cassava Flour
1 1/2 C Arrowroot Starch
1 1/4 C Crushed Potato Chips
Oil for Frying

1. Combine all of the spices into a bowl. Put half of that spice mixture into a larger bowl with the desired milk and whisk to combine.

2. Add the chicken pieces to the milk mixture then cover and allow the chicken to marinate at least 4 hours, preferably overnight.

3. When you are ready to cook the chicken combine the flours, crushed potato chips and the reserved spices into a bowl.

4. Remove the chicken from the milk bowl allowing the excess milk to drain off slightly.

5. Roll the chicken pieces into the flour fixture and set aside while you heat up the oil.

6. Preheat the oven to 400 degrees and prepare a baking sheet with a wire rack on top and set aside.

7. Bring your oil for frying up to a medium frying temp, You want the oil to have a low simmer when you put a piece of the chicken into it.

8. Fry the chicken pieces in batches until the breading is golden brown all around.

9 Transfer chicken to the baking sheet while you finish up the rest of the pieces.

10. Check the internal temperature of your pieces to ensure they are 165 degrees. If not place them into the preheated oven and allow to bake for 30-45 minutes or until the internal temperature of 165 is reached.

11. Remove from the oven, allow to cool slightly and enjoy!

Serves 4-8

Ingredients

2 lbs Boneless,
Skinless Chicken
Breasts
1 lb Ham, Thin
Sliced
1 lb Swiss Cheese,
Thin Sliced
1/4 C Coconut
Flour
1 C Tapioca Starch
1/2 C Cassava
Flour
1 1/2 TSP Garlic
Powder
1/2 TSP Salt
1/4 TSP Italian
Seasoning
2 Eggs, Large and
Slightly Beaten
2 TBS Olive Oil

Chicken Cordon Bleu
Gluten, Rice and Corn Free. (Contains Coconut).

1. Preheat the oven to 350 degrees and prepare a baking sheet with a wire rack on top of it and set it aside.

2. Place the chicken breasts between two pieces of parchment paper and hit with a meat mallet until the chicken is about 1/8 inch thick and set it aside.

3. Combine the flours and spices into a shallow dish and set aside.

4. Set the eggs into a shallow dish and set a side.

5. Take the pieces of chicken and lay them flat. Add a layer of the ham and then a layer of the cheese on top of the chicken.

6. Roll each piece of chicken into a roll, and secure the chicken with toothpicks. Repeat with remaining chicken, ham and cheese pieces.

7. Alternate the rolled chicken pieces between the egg and flour mixture to coat and set aside.

8 In a skillet add the olive oil over medium heat. Sear the outsides of the chicken breading in the pan until each piece is slightly golden brown.

9. Transfer the pieces to the prepared baking sheet and bake for about 30 minutes until the chicken is cooked all the way through, 165 degrees.

10. Allow to cool slightly, and enjoy!

Serves 4-6

Ingredients

1 lb Boneless, Skinless Chicken Breasts, Cut into 1 in Pieces
2 TBS Olive Oil
1/2 Yellow Onion, Diced
2 Cloves Garlic, Minced
1 TSP Salt
1/2 TSP Paprika
2 C Broccoli, Fresh, Chopped
4 OZ Cream Cheese
1/2 C Milk of Choice
2 C Cheddar Cheese, Shredded
4 C Cauliflower, Riced

Cheesy Chicken and Cauliflower Rice Skillet

Gluten, Tree Nut, Rice and Corn Free. (Contains Dairy)

1. In a skillet over medium heat add the olive oil and the chicken and cook, turning often until the chicken is cooked through,

2. Add the onions and allow to become slightly translucent, then add the broccoli.

3. Add the milk, cream cheese and spices and allow to simmer about 5 minutes.

4. Add the riced cauliflower and the cheese and simmer and additional 5 minutes. *Do not over cook at this point, you do not want the cauliflower to become overly soft so it retains the slight crunch like rice.*

5. Allow to cool slightly and enjoy!

Serves 4-6

Cheesy Tex-Mex Casserole

Gluten, Tree Nut, Rice and Corn Free. (Contains Dairy).

Ingredients

1 lb Boneless, Skinless Chicken Breasts cut into 1/2 inch pieces
2 TBS Avocado Oil
1 1/2 C Milk of Choice
1 C Chicken Stock
4 Oz Cream Cheese
1 C Diced Tomatoes
1 Jalapeño, Seeded and Minced
1/2 Onion, Small Diced
1/8 C Tapioca Starch
1 TBS Garlic Powder
1 1/2 TSP Salt
1 TSP Paprika
1 TSP Ancho Chili Powder
1/2 TSP Cumin
1/2 TSP Mexican Oregano
2 Batches Cassava Flour Tortillas or 8 GF Tortillas of Choice
4 C Cheddar Cheese, Shredded

1. Preheat the oven to 375 degrees.

2. In a skillet over medium heat add the avocado oil and the chicken and allow to cook, stirring occasionally until the chicken is cooked through.

3. Add the onion and jalapeño and sauté until the onion becomes translucent.

4. Add the tapioca starch and spices to the chicken and stir until combined and no excess flour remains.

5. Add the milk, chicken stock, cream cheese, diced tomatoes and spices and allow to simmer about 5 minutes until the mixture combines, then set aside.

6. In a 9x13 baking dish place a thin layer of the meat mixture. Tear up the tortillas into more bite-sized pieces and add a thin layer onto the top of the meat mixture. Add a layer of cheese and repeat until the all the ingredients have been use and the pan is filled.

7. Top with a layer of cheese and bake in the oven 30-45 min until the sauce is bubbly and the cheese has browned slightly.

8. Allow to cool slightly and enjoy!

Serves 4-8

Ingredients

2 lbs Boneless, Skinless Chicken Breasts
1/4 C 100% Agave Tequila
1/8 C Avocado Oil
5 Limes, Juiced + 1 TBS Lime Zest + 1 Lime Sliced
1/2 C Lemon Juice
1 Jalapeño, Seeded and Minced
2 Cloves Garlic, Minced
1 TSP Salt
1 TSP Ancho Chili Powder
1 TSP Mexican Oregano
1/2 TSP Cumin
1/4 TSP Onion Powder
Fresh Cilantro, Chopped

Tequila Lime Chicken
Gluten, Tree Nut, Rice, Corn and Dairy Free

1. In a large bowl or Ziploc bag combine all of the ingredients minus the chicken and mix until combined.

2. Add the chicken and allow it to marinate for at least 30 minutes up to overnight.

3. Preheat oven to 375 degrees.

4. Place the marinated chicken into a shallow baking dish and bake for 30-45 minutes until the chicken has reached 165 degrees.

5. Allow to cool slightly and enjoy!

Serve with my Mexican Cauliflower "Rice" on pg 87 or in my Tortillas on pg 121.

Serves 4-6

Ingredients

4 TBS Olive Oil, Divided
2 Boneless, Skinless Chicken Breasts, Cut into 1 inch Pieces
1 lb Andouille Sausage
1 lb Raw Shrimp, Peeled and De-veined
1 Green Bell Pepper, Cored and Rough Diced
2 Ribs of Celery, Chopped
1 Yellow Onion, Small Chopped
1 Jalapeño, Seeded and Minced
3 Cloves of Garlic, Minced
1 Can Crushed Tomatoes, 14 oz
2 C Chicken Broth
4 C Cauliflower, Riced
1 1/2 TBS Creole Seasoning
1/4 TSP Cheyenne Pepper
1 TSP Thyme
1 Bay Leaf
1/2 TSP Salt
1/2 C Okra, Thinly Sliced

Cauliflower Rice Jambalaya
Gluten, Tree Nut, Rice, Corn and Diary Free.

1. In a very large heavy bottomed skillet add the olive oil, chicken and sausage. Stir occasionally until the chicken is cooked through and the sausage has started to brown. Remove from the pan and set aside.

2. Add the remaining olive oil, and the peppers, onion, jalapeño and garlic. Sauté for about 5 minutes until the vegetables have softened and the onions have turned translucent.

3. To the skillet add the crushed tomatoes, chicken stock and the spices. Bring this to a simmer and then reduce the heat to medium and allow it to simmer about 20 minutes till the sauce has reduced by almost half.

4. Add the cauliflower, shrimp, and okra and simmer until the shrimp is cooked and pink.

5. Add the chicken and sausage back in and stir to combine.

6. Add additional spices if more heat is needed, and enjoy!

Serves 4-6

Jerk Chicken

Gluten, Rice, Corn and Dairy Free. (Nut Free Options).

Ingredients

2 lbs Chicken Pieces, Cuts of Choice
1 Yellow Onion, Small Chopped
2 Scallions, Chopped
1-2 Scotch Bonnet Chili Peppers, Stems and seeds, removed. (Depending how hot you like things.)
1/2 TSP Chinese Five-Spice Powder
1 TSP Allspice
1 TSP Black Pepper
1 TSP Thyme
1 TSP Nutmeg
1/2 TSP Paprika
1/4 TSP Lemon Grass
1 TSP Salt
1/2 C Coconut Aminos or GF Soy Sauce
1 TBS Avocado Oil

Prepare the Chicken:
1. In a food processor combine all the ingredients except the chicken. Pulse until combined.

2. Add the chicken pieces into a large bowl or Ziploc bag. Add the spice mixture to the chicken and coat.

3. Allow the chicken to sit in the spice mixture at least 30 minutes or overnight in the fridge.

To Cook:
1. Allow the chicken to come slightly to room temperature.

2. Heat the grill to medium-high heat and grill the chicken, rotating half way until cooked through, about 15-20 minutes.

3. Allow to cool slightly and enjoy!

Alternative Cooking Method:
1. preheat the oven to 400 degrees. Place the chicken onto a wire rack on a baking sheet. Bake the chicken in the oven for about 45 minutes until completely done and the internal temperature reaches 165 degrees.

Serves 4-6

Enchiladas

Gluten, Tree Nut, Rice and Corn Free. (Contains Dairy).

1. Preheat the oven to 325 degrees.

2. In a dutch oven over medium heat add the avocado oil and onion and allow them to cook until the onions start to become translucent, add minced garlic if using.

3. Add remaining ingredients except the tortillas and the cheese, bring to a low simmer for about 5 minutes.

4. Cover and transfer the Dutch oven to the oven and allow to cook 2-4 hours until the chicken is fork tender and pulls apart easily.

5. Allow to cool slightly in order to be able to handle.

6. Pull about a cup of sauce from the Dutch over and set aside. Take about 2 TBS of the sauce and spread it around the bottom of a 9x13 baking dish and set aside.

7. Shred the chicken into the remaining sauce mixture.

8. With your warmed tortillas place about 1/4 cup of the chicken mixture onto the tortilla with about 1 TBS cheese and roll to close. Place the rolled tortillas into the prepared baking dish. Repeat with remaining tortillas and chicken mixture.

9. Increase the oven temperature to 375 degrees.

10. Top the rolled tortillas in the baking pan with the reserved sauce, add an additional layer of cheese and bake about 30 minutes until the cheese has fully melted and become slightly golden.

11. Allow to cool slightly and enjoy!

This pairs well my Mexican Cauliflower "Rice" on pg 87.

Ingredients

1 Batch GF Tortillas of Choice, Warmed
2-4 C Cheddar Cheese, Shredded
2 lbs Boneless, Skinless Chicken Breasts
1/2 Yellow Onion, Diced
2 TBS Avocado Oil
1/2 C Tomato Paste
1 C Tomato Sauce
1 1/2 C Chicken Stock
1 C Chopped Tomatoes
3 Garlic Cloves, Minced or 2 TBS Garlic Powder
1 TSP Salt
1 TSP Ancho Chili Powder
1 TSP Mexican Oregano
1/2 TSP Cumin
1/4 TSP Onion Powder

Serves 4-6

Ingredients

1-2 lbs Lean
Ground Beef or
Turkey
4 TBS Olive Oil,
Divided
1/2 Yellow Onion,
Diced
1 Green Bell
Pepper, Cored and
Diced
3 Cloves Garlic, or
1 1/2 TSP Powdered
1 C Chicken Stock
1/2 C Tomato Paste
1 TSP Coconut
Aminos or GF Soy
Sauce
1/4 C Dark Brown
Sugar
1 1/2 TSP Dijon
Mustard
1 1/2 TSP Salt
1 TSP Paprika
4 Medium Sweet
Potatoes

Optional:
1 C Cheddar
Cheese, Shredded

Sweet Potato Joe's
Gluten,, Rice, and Corn Free. (Nut Free/ Dairy Free Options).

1. Preheat the oven to 400 degrees.

2. Wash and dry the sweet potatoes, brush with half the olive oil and sprinkle with salt. Wrap in foil and place in baking dish and bake for about 30-45 minutes until the sweet potatoes become fork tender.

3. While the sweet potatoes are baking prepare the filling.

4. In a skillet over medium heat cook the ground beef, or meat of choice until cooked through. Drain any excess fat if needed.

5. Add the remaining olive oil, onion and green bell pepper to the meat and continue to cook until the onions become translucent and the bell peppers become soft and start to char about 10 minutes.

6. Add remaining ingredients to the meat and vegetables minus the cheese and let the mixture simmer 5-10 minutes. Set the mixture aside until the potatoes are done cooking.

7. Once the sweet potatoes are done remove them from the oven, slice and fluff the flesh creating a little well inside the sweet potatoes.

8. Fill with the meat and vegetable mixture, top with cheese if desired and enjoy!

Serves 4-6

Chicken Fried Steak

Gluten, Rice and Corn Free. (Diary Free Options., Contains Coconut).

Ingredients

For the Steak:
2 C Buttermilk or Milk of Choice
1-2 lbs Cube Steak
1 C Cassava Flour
1/2 C Arrowroot Starch
1/2 C Coconut Flour
1 TBS Garlic Powder
1/2 TSP Salt
1 TSP Black Pepper
1 TSP Poultry Seasoning
Oil for Frying

For the Gravy:
1/2 LB Sausage
1/4 C Arrowroot Starch
2 C Milk of Choice
1 TBS Garlic Powder
1/2 TSP Salt
1 TBS Black Pepper
1 TBS Poultry Seasoning

For the Steak

1. Place the cube steak and the buttermilk into a bowl. Cover and allow to chill for about 15-20 minutes. The buttermilk will help to tenderize the cube steak as well as helping the breading adhere to the steak.

2. Place the spices into a bowl with the flours into a shallow dish.

3. Once the meat has soaked dredge the meat into the flour mixture until fully coated. You can do this more than once to get a thicker coating if that's desired.

4. Fry the steak pieces in desired oil about 4-5 minutes per side until the steak is done and the coating is golden brown. Set aside on a plate of towels to allow the excess oils to drain off while you cook the remaining pieces.

For the Gravy

1. Cook the sausage of choice until it is browned.

2. Add the arrowroot starch until the sausage is coated.

3. Add milk of choice and spices and then simmer until it has thickened, about 10 minutes.

Serves 4-6

Beef Tips and Gravy

Gluten, Tree Nut, Rice and Corn Free. (Dairy Free Options).

Ingredients:

1 2-4 lb Beef Roast of Choice, Cubed into about 1 in Pieces
1 Yellow Onion
2 Cups Baby Portobello Mushrooms
2 TBS Olive Oil
4 C Beef Stock
4 Cloves of garlic, chopped or 2 TBS Ground
1 TBS Salt
1 TSP Basil
1 TSP Oregano
1 TSP Thyme
4 TBS Butter or Ghee
1/4 C Tapioca or Arrowroot Starch
1/4 C Milk of Choice

1. Dice the roast into 1 inch pieces, slice the onions and mushrooms.

2. If using a Dutch oven preheat your oven to 275 degrees or you can use a crock-pot set on low. (If using a crock-pot brown your meat and veggies on the stove before adding them to the crock-pot.)

3 If using a Dutch oven you can brown the meat and then transfer it to the oven.

4. Brown the meat and veggies until they have started to caramelize and the meat has some color. Transfer if needed.

5. To the meat and veggies mixture add the olive oil, half the beef stock and spices. Cook in the Dutch Oven at 275 degrees for about 3-4 hours or in the crock-pot on low. The meat will be fall apart tender when done.

6. Once the meat is cooked add the butter, or ghee, and flour until the meat is coated and no lumps of flour remain.

7. Add the remaining beef stock and milk of choice and allow to simmer on the stove over medium heat until the sauce starts to thicken, about 5 minutes. If you are using the crock-pot you can either transfer the sauce to a pan on the stove or increase temperature to high for about 15 minutes.

8. Serve over your favorite potatoes or rice, and enjoy!

Serves 4-6

Maple Dijon Chicken

Gluten, Dairy, Rice and Corn Free. (Nut Free Options).

Ingredients

1-2 lbs Boneless, Skinless Chicken Breasts
1 TBS Tapioca Starch
1/2 C Dijon Mustard
1/2 C Pure Maple Syrup
1 TBS Coconut Aminos or GF Soy Sauce
1/2 TSP Salt
1 TSP Garlic Powder
2 TSP Thyme

1. Preheat the oven to 375 degrees.

2. Place the chicken into a 9x13 baking dish and set aside.

3. Add the remaining ingredients into a small bowl and whisk until combined.

4. Coat the chicken in the sauce reserving 1/4 of it aside.

5. Bake the chicken in the oven for 30-45 minutes until the chicken reaches 165 degrees and is cooked through.

6. Remove from the oven, drizzle with remaining sauce if desired and enjoy.

Serves 4-6

CHAPTER 4

NICE RICE

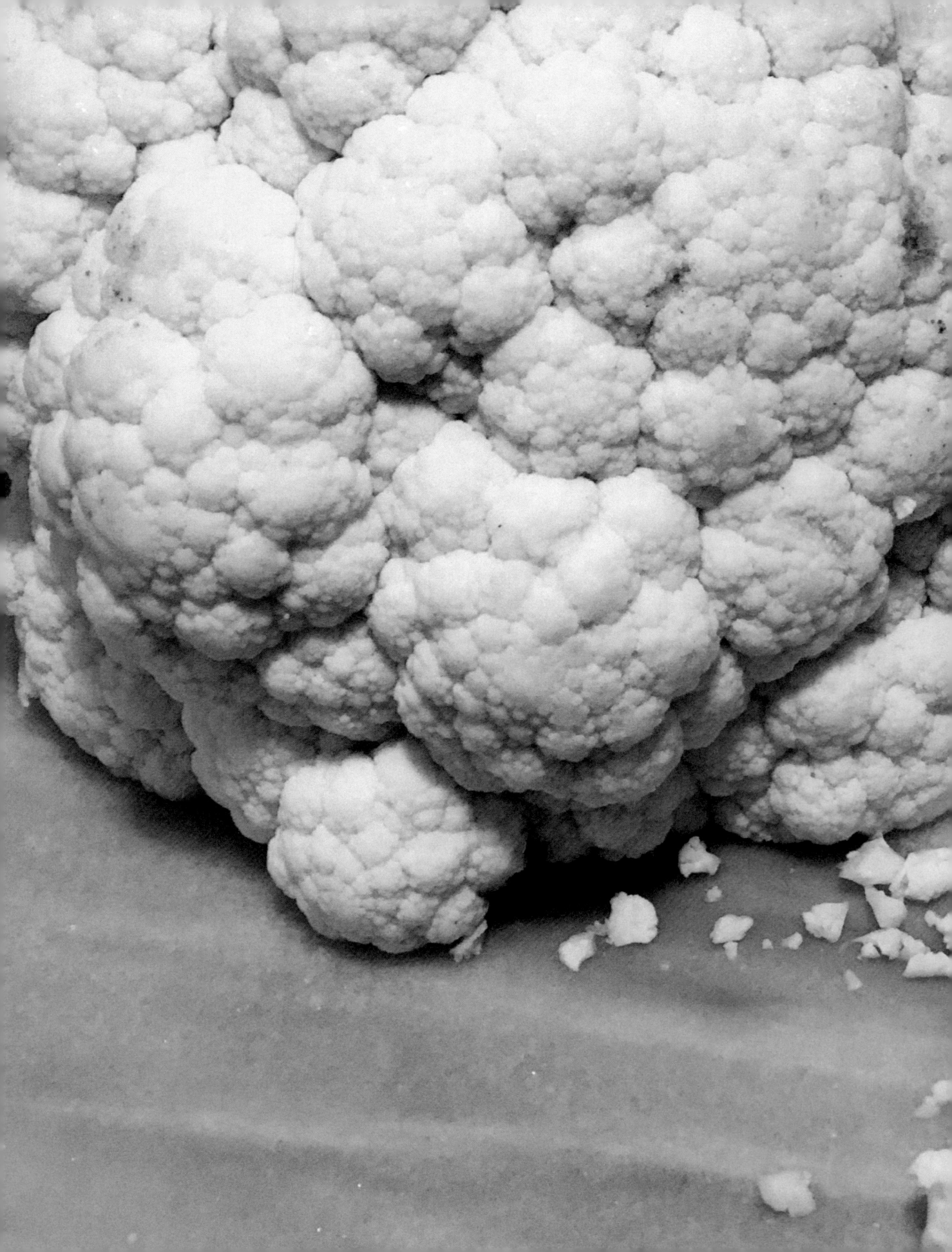

Ingredients

1 Head Cauliflower
1/2 TSP Salt
1/2 TSP Garlic
Powder
1 TBS Avocado Oil or
Olive Oil

Classic Cauliflower "Rice"
Gluten, Tree Nut, Rice , Corn and Diary Free.

1. Wash and rough chop the head of cauliflower.

2. Add the cauliflower to the bowl of a food processor and pulse until rice consistency. Do not over pulse.

3. In a skillet over medium heat add the oil and cauliflower. Sauté the riced cauliflower until slightly crisp but tender, about 5 minutes.

4. Add spices, stir and serve in place of traditional rice with all your favorite dishes!

Serves 4-6

Pesto Broccoli "Rice"

Gluten, Rice, Corn Free. (Contains Nuts and Dairy).

Ingredients

1 Large Broccoli Crown
1 C Fresh Basil
1 TBS Pine Nuts
2 Cloves Garlic
1/4 C Olive Oil + 1 TBS Set Aside
1/4 C Parmesan Cheese, Grated
1/2 TSP Salt

1. Wash and rough chop the broccoli crown. Place the broccoli into the bowl of a food processor and pulse until rice consistency is achieved. Do not over pulse, set aside.

2. In a small food processor add the remaining ingredients and pulse until smooth, set aside.

3. In a skillet over medium heat add the olive oil and broccoli and stir occasionally about 5 minutes.

4. Add the pest sauce to the broccoli and stir occasionally until the sauce is warm about 2-3 minutes.

5. Allow to cool slightly and enjoy!

Serves 4-6

Cauliflower Fried "Rice"

Gluten, Rice, Corn and Dairy Free. (Nut Free Options).

Ingredients

1 Head Cauliflower
1 TBS Sesame Oil
1/8 C Coconut Aminos or GF Soy Sauce
1 Egg, Large
1/2 TSP Salt
2 Cloves Garlic, Minced or 2 TSP Garlic Powder
1/2 Onion, Small Diced
1/2 C Peas
1/2 C Carrots, Small Diced
3 Scallions, Thinly Sliced

1. Wash and rough chop the head of cauliflower. Place the cauliflower into the bowl of a food processor and pulse until rice consistency is achieved. Do not over pulse, set aside.

2. In a skillet over medium heat add the sesame oil onion and carrots. Sauté until the onion becomes translucent and the carrots are fork tender.

3. Push the onion and carrot mixture to the side of the pan. Pace the egg on the other side and let it cook. As the begins to finish cooking, break it up and continue to let it cook. Mix into the onion and carrot mix.

4. Add the peas and cauliflower to the skillet and cook, stirring occasionally, about 5 minutes.

5. Add the coconut aminos or soy sauce, spices and scallions and stir.

6. Allow to cool slightly and enjoy along side your favorite dish!

Serves 4-6

Ingredients

1 Head Cauliflower
1/4 C Butter or Ghee
1/8 C Tapioca Starch
2 C Milk of Choice
1 1/2 TSP Garlic Powder
1 TSP Salt
1/2 TSP Paprika
1/2 TSP Thyme
1 1/2 C Cheddar Cheese, Shredded

Cheesy Cauliflower "Rice"

Gluten, Tree Nut, Rice and Corn Free (Contains Diary).

1. Wash and trim the head of cauliflower.

2. Rough chop the cauliflower and place into the bowl of a food processor and pulse until the consistency of rice. Do not over pulse, set aside.

3. In a medium sized saucepan over medium heat melt the putter.

4. Once the butter is melted add the tapioca starch until a paste forms.

5. Add milk of choice to saucepan and whisk till combined.

6. Add the riced cauliflower to the pan and simmer till the sauce thickens about 5 minutes. (Do not over cook).

7. Add the spies and cheese then stir until the cheese is completely melted.

8. Allow to slightly cool, serve and enjoy!

Serves 4-6

Mexican Cauliflower "Rice"

Gluten, Dairy, Rice, Corn and Dairy Free.

1. Wash and rough chop the cauliflower. Place the cauliflower into the bowl of a food processor and pulse until rice consistency is achieved, set aside.

2. Heat avocado oil in a skillet oven medium heat and add the chicken broth, tomato paste and spices to the skillet.

3. Bring to a simmer and let the sauce reduce.

4. Add the cauliflower, stirring occasionally, about 3 minutes.

5. Allow to cool slightly and serve along side your favorite dish and enjoy!

1 Head Cauliflower
2 TBS Avocado Oil
8 oz Tomato Paste
1/2 C Chicken Broth
1 TSP Chili Powder
1 TSP Garlic Powder
1 TSP Salt

Serves 4-6

Ingredients

1 Head Cauliflower
2 TBS Butter or Ghee
1/2 Yellow Onion, Small, Diced
2 Cloves Garlic, Minced or 1 TSP Powdered
1 TSP Turmeric
1/2 C Chicken Stock
1 Bay Leaf
1/2 TSP Thyme
1/2 TSP Salt

Turmeric Cauliflower "Rice"
Gluten, Tree Nut, Rice and Corn Free. (Dairy Free Options).

1. Wash and rough chop the cauliflower. Place the cauliflower into the bowl of a food processor and pulse until rice consistency is achieved, set aside.

2. Melt the butter in a skillet over medium heat, add the onions and garlic and sauté about 5 minutes.

3. Add the spices and chicken stock and simmer another 5 minutes.

4. Add cauliflower to the sauce and stir until coated. Continue to cook about 5 minutes while stirring often.

5. Allow to cool slightly and enjoy!

Serves 4-6

Mushroom "Risotto"

Gluten, Tree Nut, Rice and Corn Free. (Contains Dairy).

Ingredients

1 Head Cauliflower
2 TBS Olive Oil
1/2 Onion, Small Diced
1 C Portabella Mushrooms, Sliced
2 Cloves Garlic or 1 TBS Ground
1/2 C Chicken Broth
1/8 C Heavy Cream
1/4 C Parmesan Cheese
1/4 C Mozzarella Cheese
1 TSP Salt

Optional:
2 TBS Parsley, Chopped

1. Wash and rough chop the head of cauliflower. Place into the bowl of a food processor and pulse until the consistency. Do not over pulse.

2. In a skillet over medium heat add the olive oil, diced onion, mushrooms and garlic. Saute until the onions have become translucent and the mushrooms have slightly browned.

3. Add the chicken broth, heavy cream and salt. Bring to a low simmer.

4. Add the cauliflower and allow to cook, stirring occasionally about 5 min.

5. Remove from heat, stir in cheese and salt and stir until melted.

6. Top with parsley if desired and enjoy!

Serves 4-6

CHAPTER 5

VEGGIES

Ingredients

2 lbs Green Beans
1/8 C Olive Oil
2 Cloves Garlic,
Minced or 1 TBS
Ground
1 TSP Salt
1/2 TSP White
Pepper
Juice from 1
Lemon + 1 TBS
Lemon Zest
1/3 C Parmesan
Cheese, Grated

Optional:
2 TBS Pine Nuts,
Toasted

Parmesan Roasted Green Beans
Gluten, Dairy, Rice and Corn Free. (Nut Free Options).

1. Preheat the oven to 400 degrees and line a baking sheet with parchment paper, set aside.

2. Wash and trim green beans and lay on the prepared baking sheet.

3. In a small bowl combine the olive oil, garlic, spices and lemon juice and whisk until combined.

4. Toss the green beans with half of the sauce mixture, reserving the other half for later.

5. Roast the green beans for about 30 minutes until the beans have started to brown slightly.

6. Remove the green beans from the oven, top with the lemon zest, Parmesan cheese and pine nuts if desired and enjoy!

Serves 4-6

Honey Sriracha Carrots

Gluten, Tree Nut, Rice, Corn and Dairy Free

Ingredients

2 lbs Carrots. Sliced
1/4 C Honey
1/8 C Sriracha Sauce
1 TSP Salt
1/2 TSP Garlic Powder
1 TBS Avocado Oil

1. Preheat the oven to 400 degrees and line a baking sheet with parchment paper and set aside.

2. Wash, peel and slice carrots and place on prepared baking sheet.

3. Combine the remaining ingredients into a small bowl and whisk together.

4. Drizzle and toss the carrots with the sauce to coat.

5. Roast the carrots about 30 minutes until fork tender and sauce has caramelized over the carrots.

6. Remove from oven, allow to cool slightly and enjoy!

Serves 4-6

Ingredients

1 - 2 lb mini potatoes, or regular if you want bigger ones.
2 TBS Olive Oil
1/4 C Butter or Ghee, Melted
1 TSP Salt
1 TSP Garlic Powder
2 C Cheddar Cheese, Shredded

Optional Toppings:
Sour Cream
1 C Cooked Bacon, Chopped
Green Onions. Chopped

Loaded Hasselback Potatoes
Gluten, Tree Nut, Rice and Corn Free. (Contains Dairy).

1. Preheat the oven to 400 degrees and line a baking sheet with parchment paper and set aside.

2. Wash and dry the potatoes. With a small knife cut the potato into thin slices, making sure to not cut all the way through, leaving the potatoes in tack. This will allow the potatoes to fan out a little bit and fall open.

3. Place the potatoes on the baking sheet. Combine the butter, olive oil and spices into a small bow. Brush the tops of the potatoes with the mixture.

4. Bake the potatoes for about 30 minutes. until they are fork tender.

5. Remove the potatoes from the oven, top with cheese and then return them to the oven to bake an additional 10-15 minutes until the cheese is melted and slightly golden.

6. Remove the potatoes from oven once the cheese is melted and allow to cool for 5 minutes before topping with the sour cream, chopped bacon and green onions as desired and enjoy!

Serves 4-6

Whole Roasted Cauliflower

Gluten, Tree Nut, Rice and Corn Free. (Dairy Free Options).

Ingredients

1 Whole Head of Cauliflower, trimmed and clean, left whole.
1 C of Mayo
2 Cloves Garlic, Smashed, Chopped
1/4 C Grated Onion
1 TSP Salt
1/2 TSP Paprika
1/2 TSP Thyme
1/4 TSP Rosemary

Optional:
1 C Cheddar Cheese

1. Preheat the oven to 400 degrees.

2. Clean, trim and slightly core the head of cauliflower and place it in a lightly greased baking pan. I usually use my 8x8 glass dish for this.

3. Place the remaining ingredients into a bowl and mix until combined.

4. Spread the mixture over the top of the cauliflower and let it rest about 5-10 minutes.

5. Lightly tent over the cauliflower with a piece of foil and bake the cauliflower for about 30 minutes.

6. Remove the foil and continue to bake for an additional 15-20 minutes until the cauliflower has reached a golden color and is fork tender.

7. Slice up and enjoy!

Serves 4-6

Balsamic Broccolini and Mushrooms

Gluten, Tree Nut, Rice, Corn and Dairy Free

1. Preheat oven to 400 degrees. Line a sheet pan with parchment paper and set aside.

2. Wash, dry and arrange the broccolini, mushrooms and cheery tomatoes onto the baking sheet.

3. In a small bowl whisk together the remaining ingredients.

4. Drizzle the sauce over the vegetables and toss the vegetables to coat completely.

5. Roast the vegetables for about 25-30 minutes until they have started to change colors and they are fork tender.

6. Let cool slightly and enjoy!

Ingredients

1 lb Broccolini
2 C Portabella Mushrooms, Sliced
1 C Cheery Tomatoes, Sliced
1/4 C Balsamic Vinegar
1/2 C Olive Oil
2 Cloves of Garlic. or 1 TBS Powdered
1 TSP Pink Salt
1 TSP Thyme
1 TSP Oregano
1 TSP Basil

Serves 4-6

Roasted Lemon Garlic Broccoli

Gluten, Tree Nut, Rice, Corn and Dairy Free

Ingredients

1 1/2 lbs Broccoli, about 4 C
1/2 C Avocado Oil or Olive Oil
1 Lemon Juiced + 1 TBS Lemon Zest
1 TSP Garlic Powder
1 TSP Salt

1. Preheat the oven to 400 degrees and prepare a baking sheet lined with parchment paper.

2. Wash and rough chop the broccoli. and place it onto the baking sheet. I like to split some of the larger pieces in half so they can lay flatter on the pan.

3. Combine the remaining ingredients minus the lemon zest into a small bowl and whisk until combined.

4. Drizzle the mixture onto the broccoli and toss around to coat. Reserving about 1 TBS aside.

5. Roast the broccoli for about 30-45 min until it is fork tender and the broccoli ends have started to change colors.

6. Drizzle with remaining mixture and top with lemon zest and enjoy!

Serves 4-6

Ingredients

2 lbs Yellow
Potatoes
1/4 C Butter or
Ghee + 1 TBS
1/4 Tapioca
Starch
1 1/2 C Milk of
Choice or Half
and Half
1 TSP Salt
1 1/2 TSP Garlic
Powder
1 TSP Paprika
1/2 TSP Thyme
2 C Cheddar
Cheese + 1/4 C
Set Aside

Optional:
2 TBS Parsley

Scalloped Potatoes
Gluten, Tree Nut, Rice and Corn Free. (Dairy Free Options).

1. Preheat the oven to 350 degrees and grease a 9x13 baking dish with the 1 TBS of butter.

2. Wash, dry and peel the potatoes, then thinly slice to about 1/16 to an 1/8 of an inch thick. Set aside on some paper towels to allow extra water to drain out of the potatoes. A mandolin slicer or a food processor can make this job easier.

3. In a saucepan over medium heat melt the remaining butter. Once the butter is melted whisk in the tapioca starch until completely combined and a paste is formed.

4. Stir in the milk of choice and whisk often until the mixture starts to thicken, about 5 minutes.

5. Remove from heat and stir in the cheese and spices, whisk until combined and set aside.

6. Start layering the potatoes into the bottom of the 9x13 pan. Spoon about 1/4 of the sauce over the layer of potatoes. Repeat with remaining potatoes and sauce until they are gone and pan is filled.

7. Top with reserved cheese and bake for about 45 minutes to an hour until the potatoes are fork tender, the sauce is bubbly and the cheese is slightly golden.

8. Allow to cool slightly, top with parsley if desired and enjoy!

Serves 4-6

Asian Roasted Broccoli and Carrots

Gluten, Rice, Corn and Dairy Free. (Nut Free Options).

1. Preheat oven to 400 degrees and prepare a baking sheet with parchment paper, set aside.

2. Wash and prepare the broccoli and carrots into chunks and slices.

3. Combine the remaining ingredients minus the sesame seeds into a saucepan over medium and whisk till combined. Bring the mixture to a simmer and allow to thicken about 5-10 minutes.

4. Drizzle 3/4 of the mixture over the broccoli and carrots, setting the rest aside.

5. Roast the broccoli and carrots for about 30-45 min until they are fork tender and their color starts to turn a little.

6. Remove from the oven, toss with remaining sauce and sesame seeds if desired and enjoy!

Ingredients

1 Head of Broccoli, Chopped
1 lb Carrots, Sliced
1/4 C Coconut Amiinos or GF Soy Sauce
2 TBS Dark Brown Sugar
1 TBS Sesame Oil
1 TSP Apple Cider Vinegar
1 TBS Sriracha Sauce
3 Cloves of Garlic, Minced or 2 TBS Powdered
1/2 TSP Salt

Optional:
1 TBS Sesame Seeds

Serves 4-6

Greek Potatoes

Gluten, Tree Nut, Rice, Corn and Dairy Free.

Ingredients

1-2 lb White, Yellow or Red Potatoes
1/2 C Mayo
1 TBS Olive Oil
2 Cloves Garlic, Chopped or 1 TBS Ground
Juice from 2 Lemons + 1 TBS Lemon Zest
1 TSP Rosemary
1 TSP Oregano
1 TSP Salt
1/2 TSP Thyme

1. Preheat the oven to 400 degrees. Prepare a baking sheet with parchment paper and set it aside.

2. Wash, dry and chop the potatoes into about 1./2 inch pieces.

3. Combine the remaining ingredients into a bowl minus the lemon zest and whisk till combined.

4. Place the potatoes on the baking sheet, drizzle and coat the potatoes with the sauce and roast them for about 45 minutes until the potatoes have started to turn a golden color and are fork tender. Make sure to occasionally rotate the potatoes about halfway to make sure that they crisp all the way around on all edges.

5. Remove the potatoes from the oven and top them with lemon set zest and enjoy!

Serves 4-6

Ingredients

I Head of
Cauliflower
1/4 C Honey
1/4 Sriracha
2 TBS Avocado Oil
1 TBS Coconut
Aminos or GF Soy
Sauce
1 TSP Salt
1 TSP Garlic
Powder

Sweet and Spicy Smashed Cauliflower

Gluten, Dairy, Rice and Corn Free. (Nut Free Options).

1. Preheat the oven to 400 degrees and prepare a baking sheet lined with parchment paper.

2. Wash, trim and rough chop the head of cauliflower.

3. In a bowl or large Ziploc bag combine the cauliflower and remaining ingredients and toss to fully coat the cauliflower in the mixture. Allow to sit about 5 minutes and toss again.

4. Spread the cauliflower onto the prepared baking sheet, do not over crowd the pieces.

5. Bake the cauliflower for about 30 minutes until it is fork tender and has started to turn a slight golden color.

6 Pull the cauliflower from the oven and using the back of a fork or a potato masher, push down onto the cauliflower pieces to flatten them.

7. Once you have smashed the cauliflower, flip the pieces over and return the pan to the oven. Bake for an additional 10-15 minutes until the cauliflower has started to turn colors and the edges have crisped.

8. Serve along side your favorite dinner and enjoy!

Serves 4-6

Classic Mashed Cauliflower

Gluten, Tree Nut, Rice and Corn Free. (Diary Free Options).

1 Large Head of Cauliflower
4 TBS Butter for Ghee
1 TSP Garlic Powder
1/2 TSP Salt

1. Clean, trim and slightly core the head of cauliflower but leave it whole if possible.

2. In a saucepan, preferably with a strainer insert place the cauliflower in to steam over medium-high heat until the cauliflower becomes more than fork tender.

3. Once the cauliflower becomes very tender place it in a colander and allow as much water to drain out as possible. I usually let mine sit about 10 minutes while I work on something else for dinner. You can slightly press down with the back of a spoon to help it drain as well.

4. Once the cauliflower has drained transfer it to the bowl of a food processor along with the remaining ingredients.

5. Process in the food processor on high until the cauliflower has become silky smooth and no clumps of cauliflower remain.

6. Serve in the place of your traditional mashed potatoes and enjoy!

Note: Steaming the cauliflower may require adding additional water under the basket as it steams depending on your set up.

You may place it directly into the water if you do not have a basket but it will require additional draining so the end result does not end up overly watery.

Serves 4-6

Honey Brown Butter Carrots

Gluten, Tree Nut, Rice and Corn Free. (Dairy Free Options).

Ingredients

1-2 lbs carrots, sliced
4 TBS Butter or Ghee
1 TBS Honey
1/2 TSP Garlic Powder
1/4 TSP Pink Salt

Optional:
Fresh Parsley for topping

1. Preheat the oven to 375 degrees and prepare a baking sheet with parchment paper.

2. Place the carrots on the baking sheet and set aside.

3. In a saucepan over low heat place the butter or ghee and allow it to simmer. Whisk the butter until it turns a golden brown, but not to dark. This should take about 5-10 minutes.

4. Remove the saucepan from the heat once the butter has the nice almost hazelnut coloring to it. Stir in the honey, garlic and salt until the honey is completely combined into the butter.

5. Coat the carrots in the butter mixture and bake in the oven for about 25-35 minutes, rotating once halfway.

6. The carrots are done when they are desired fork tender.

7. Top with fresh chopped parsley if desired and enjoy!

Serves 4-6

CHAPTER 6

BREADS

Ingredients

1/3 C Olive Oil
1 C Milk or Water
2 Eggs, Large
2 C Arrowroot Starch
1 C Cassava Flour
1/2 TSP Garlic Powder
1/4 TSP Salt
1 C Shredded Cheese of Choice

Pizza Crust
Gluten, Tree Nut, Rice and Corn Free

1. In the bowl of a stand mixer combine the olive oil, milk and eggs and mix on medium speed until combined.

2. Next to the bowl of the mixer add the cassava flour and the arrowroot starch, along with the spices.

3. Finally add your one cup of shredded cheese to the mixer and mix until a ball of dough forms.

4. Preheat the oven to 450 degrees.

5. While the oven is preheating place a piece of parchment paper onto a pizza pan, add the dough press the crust into the desired shape and thickness.

6. Once the dough is rolled out and the oven is preheated, place the crust into the oven and pre-bake the crust for about 12-15 minutes depending on the thickness.

7. Once the pizza is done pre-baking, pull it out of the oven, top it with desired toppings and bake an additional 10-12 minutes until the toppings are cooked and the cheese is slightly golden.

8. Once the pizza is done, pull it out of the oven and let the pizza cool for about 5 minutes, slice and enjoy!

Note: I use cheddar cheese as it gives a slight yeasty flavor.

Use fresh shredded cheese for this for the best result.

This crust is a thinner style crust so if you want it thicker roll less and then adjust the cooking time.

Yield 1 Large 14 Inch Pizza

Ingredients

1 C Warm Water
2 1/4 TSP Yeast
3 Egg Whites
1/8 C Sugar
1/4 C Avocado Oil
1 TBS Apple Cider Vinegar
2 C Cassava Flour
1/2 C Arrowroot Starch
1/2 C Potato Starch
1/8 C Psyllium Husk Powder
1 TSP Guar Gum
1/2 TSP Salt
1/2 TSP Baking Soda
1 TSP Cream of Tartar

Note: split the dough into two if you have smaller ones.

I have found when I insert a thermometer into the center of the bread and it reaches 205-210 degrees it yields the best results.

Classic Sandwich Bread
Gluten, Tree Nut, Dairy, Rice and Corn Free.

1. In the bowl of a stand mixer add the egg whites and whisk on high until medium peaks are formed.

2. While the eggs whites are being beaten, in a separate bowl combine the warm water and yeast and allow it to bloom about 5 minutes.

3. Once the yeast has bloomed add the sugar, avocado oil and apple cider vinegar to the yeast mixture.

4. Once the egg whites have formed medium peaks. Fold the yeast mixture into the egg whites making sure they do not completely fall.

5. In a separate bowl mix the flours, psyllium husk powder, guar gum, salt, baking soda and cream of tartar.

6. Slowly fold the flour mixture into the other ingredients in the bowl. *The dough will resemble a very thick cake batter.*

7. Line a 9x5 loaf pan or larger with parchment paper.

8. Pour the dough into the prepared loaf pan. Allow it to rest while you preheat the oven.

9. Preheat the oven to 350 degrees, Bake for 45 minutes to an hour until the top of the bread becomes a slight golden color and it springs back when you push on the top.

10. Remove the finished bread from the oven. Allow it to completely cool before removing it from loaf pan and slicing.

Yield 1 9x5 inch Loaf

Country Biscuits

Gluten, Rice and Corn Free. (Contains Coconut).

Ingredients

1 1/4 C Cassava Flour
1/2 C Arrowroot Starch
1 TBS Psyllium Husk Powder
1/8 C Sugar
1/2 TSP Baking Soda
1 TSP Cream of Tartar
1/2 TSP Salt
1/2 C Butter, Cold
2 Eggs, Large
1 C Milk of Choice

1. Preheat oven to 450 degrees.

2. Combine cassava flour, arrowroot starch, psyllium husk powder, sugar, baking soda and cream of tartar into a bowl. Whisk until combined and set aside.

3. Dice the chilled butter into small cubes and add it to the flour mixture. Using a pastry cutter, or a fork work the butter into the flour mixture until it is crumbly but not completely combined. You want to still see about pea sized portions of butter in the flour. Work fast as you want your butter to remain cold.

4. Combine the eggs and milk, into a separate bowl and whisk until combined.

5. Slowly add the wet mixture into the flour mixture and fold the two together until just combined. Be careful not to overly work the dough.

6. Lightly dust a pastry board or piece of parchment paper with arrowroot starch and place dough on surface. Lightly roll out dough until it is about an inch and half thick. Cut the biscuits with a biscuit cutter or a 2 or 3 inch cutter. Alternately you can hand form the biscuits into desired shape.

7. Place biscuits slightly touching in a greased baking pan, Cast iron or glass is fine.

8. Bake the biscuits for about 220-25 minutes until the biscuits almost double in height and have slightly browned on top.

9. Lightly brush the tops with melted butter and serve by themselves or top with some country gravy for a savory breakfast treat!

Yield 8-12 Biscuits

Crusty Bread

Gluten, Tree Nut, Rice and Corn Free. (Dairy Free Options).

Ingredients

3/4 C Warm Water
2 1/4 TSP Yeast or 1 Packet
1 TBS Sugar
2 TBS Butter or Ghee, Softened
3 Eggs, Large
1 1/4 C Cassava Flour
1 C Arrowroot Starch
1/4 C Tapioca Starch
1/2 TSP Salt

1. In the bowl of a stand mixer combine the warm water and yeast and let it bloom, about 5-10 minutes.

2. Once the yeast has bloomed at the sugar, butter or ghee and eggs to the yeast mixture. Mix on medium until it is all combined.

3. Combine the flours and salt into a separate bowl and then gradually combine the flour mixture into the wet ingredients while the mixer is on medium-low speed. The dough will start to ball up and pull away from the sides when it is done.

4. Place the dough into either a large covered dutch oven, or shape and place onto a lined baguette pan. If you do not have either you can shape into desired shape on a baking sheet covered in parchment paper.

5. Allow the dough to rise while you preheat the oven.

6. Preheat the oven to 375 degrees.

7. Once the oven has preheated bake the bread for about 20-30 min depending on size and shape that you chose. The bread will create a nice crust on the outside with a slight golden color when it is done.

8. Let the bread cool about 5 minutes, slice and enjoy!

Yield 1 Loaf

Cheese Bread

Gluten, Tree Nut, Rice and Corn Free. (Contains Dairy).

Ingredients

1 C Milk
1/2 C Oil
1/4 TSP Pink Salt
1/4 TSP Garlic Powder
2 C Tapioca Starch or Arrowroot Starch
1 C Cheddar Cheese
1/2 C Mozzarella Cheese
2 Eggs, Large

1. Preheat the oven to 375 degrees and grease a muffin tin then set it aside.

2. In a saucepan over medium heat bring the milk and oil to a low boil, then remove the pan from the heat.

3. Once removed stir in the spices and tapioca or arrowroot starch until combined. It will be a thick paste like texture.

4. Transfer this mixture to the bowl of a stand mixer and mix on medium-high until the mixture becomes smooth, about a minute.

5. While the mixer is on medium speed, slowly add the cheeses a little at time until it is all completely combined.

6. Once all the cheese is combined add the eggs and mix until combined.

7. Spoon the dough into the wells of a muffin tin about 1/3-1/2 full depending on how big you want your finished rolls.

8. Bake the balls until they fluff and become slightly golden brown, about 18- 25 minutes depending on size.

Note: You can change the cheeses out in these or add different spices to change the flavors.

I like to change to all mozzarella and add garlic and dried herbs and make little garlic balls.

This dough can be frozen and baked off later. Just make the balls, freeze then store in a Ziploc bag until you wan to bake them. Do not thaw. Just add 2-4 more minutes onto the baking times.

Yield 24-36 Bread Bites

Tortillas

Gluten, Tree Nut, Rice, Corn and Dairy Free.

Ingredients

1 3/4 C Cassava Flour
1 TSP Salt
1 TSP Garlic Powder
1 1/2 C Hot Water
3 TBS Avocado Oil
2 TBS Honey

1. In a bowl combine the hot water, avocado oil and honey and whisk until combined.

2. To the bowl add the salt, garlic powder and cassava flour.

3. Knead the dough until it forms a ball of dough.

4. If the mixture becomes crumbly and does not stay together nicely add more water a tsp at a time. If the mixture becomes too wet add a half a tsp of cassava flour to the mixture.

5. The dough should hold together nicely so when you go to roll it out it does not break on you.

6. Divide the dough into 6-8 equal sized balls of dough depending on what size you want to make your tortillas.

7. Using either a tortilla press or just two pieces of parchment paper and a rolling pin, press or roll your tortillas to your desired size.

8. Heat a skillet to about medium-low heat and lightly grease it.

9. On the skillet place one tortilla and allow it to cook until you see it start to puff a little bit and the edges start to pull away from the pan, about 1-2 minutes.

10. Flip the tortilla over and continue to cook it on the other side about the same time.

11. This step is important! When the tortillas are just off the skillet and hot place them into a tortilla warmer or on a plate covered with a clean dish towel or layers of paper towels. The tortillas need to be able to steam themselves a bit in order for them to maintain their pliability.

12. Fill them and enjoy!

Note: You want these to be thin because to do just about double in thickness once they are cooked. The thinner they are the better they roll without cracking.

Yield 8, 6 inch Tortillas

CHAPTER 7

SWEETS

Classic Chocolate Chip Cookies
Gluten, Tree Nut, Rice and Corn Free. (Contains Dairy)

Ingredients

1/2 C Sugar
1 C Dark Brown Sugar
2 Eggs, Large
2 TBS Vanilla
1/2 TSP Salt
1 C Butter, Softened
6 OZ Cream Cheese, Softened
1 TSP Baking Soda
1 TSP Guar Gum
1 TSP Salt
1 C Cassava Flour
1 1/2 C Arrowroot starch
1 12 oz Bag of Chocolate Chips of Choice

1. In the bowl of a stand mixer, cream the butter, cream cheese, sugar and brown sugar until completely combined and it is light and fluffy in appearance.

2. To the butter and sugar mixture add the eggs, and vanilla and mix until combined.

3. Next in separate bowl combine the cassava flour, arrowroot starch, baking soda, salt and guar gum.

4. Gradually combine the flour mixture into the bowl with the remaining ingredients.

5. Fold the chocolate chips into the batter.

6. Cover the dough and allow it to chill for about 30 minutes in the fridge so it is easier to handle.

7. Preheat the oven to 350 degrees.

8. Once the dough has chilled preheat the oven to 350 degrees.

9. Roll dough into about 1/8 c size balls and place on a sheet pan line with parchment paper, about 2-3 inches apart.

10. Bake at 350 degrees for about 10-12 minutes until the cookie starts to puff and the middle looks still slightly undone and the edges on the bottom start to turn a little golden brown. The dark brown sugar in these cookies will make them brown all over faster but they will still be chewy.

11. Remove the cookies from the oven and allow to cool on the sheet pan about minutes before transferring them to a cooling rack.

12. Repeat until all the dough has been cooked or portion into balls and freeze to bake at a later time. and enjoy!

Yield 24 Cookies

Note: I use Enjoy Life Brand Chocolate Chips.

Ingredients

12 Oz Dark
Chocolate
3/4 C Coconut Oil
or Sunflower Oil
1 1/3 C Sugar
2 Eggs, Large
1 TBS Vanilla
1/4 C Cocoa
Powder
1/3 C Arrowroot
Flour
1 TSP Baking Soda
1/4 TSP Salt

Option:
Extra Chocolate
Chips, nuts or
other favorites to
add into brownies.

Brownies
Gluten, Rice, Corn Free. (Diary Free / Nut Free Options).

1. Preheat the oven to 350 degrees and slightly oil an 8x8 baking dish and set it aside.

2. In a pot on the stove over medium heat, melt the chocolate and oil. Whisk until it is completely melted and combined.

3. Remove the pot from the heat and whisk in the sugar while the chocolate is hot and then add the eggs one at a time.

4. Add the vanilla to the mixture.

5. In a separate bowl combine the cocoa powder, arrowroot starch, baking soda and salt and mix them all together.

6. Slowly fold in the flour mixture into the melted chocolate mixture.

7. Pour the mixture into the preprepared baking dish and level out the mixture.

8. Bake at 350 degrees for about 18-22 minutes until a knife inserted into the middle comes out clean. *Do not over bake.*

Note: I use Enjoy Life Chocolate.

If you want this nut free sub equal sunflower or other light cooking oil for the coconut oil.

Feel free to add in additional chocolate chips or even a favorite chopped nut if you like those in your brownies.

Yield 1 8x8 Pan

Avocado Mousse

Gluten, Rice, Corn and Tree Nut Free. (Dairy Free Options).

1. Melt the chocolate and set it aside to slightly cool.

2. In a food processor combine the avocados, cooled chocolate and milk of choice. Process on high until completely smooth and no avocado lumps remain.

3. Add the remaining ingredients and continue to process until the mixture is smooth.

4. Top with your favorite whipped cream, shaved chocolates or even use as a frosting on your favorite grain free cake and enjoy!

2 Ripe Avocados
1/4 C Dark Chocolate
1/4 C Dark Cocoa Powder
1/3 C Milk of Choice
1/4 Honey or Sugar or Sweetener of Choice
1/4 TSP Vanilla Extract
1/8 TSP Salt

Note: I use Enjoy Life chocolate.

This recipe requires perfectly soft, ripe avocados.

Yield 2 Cups

Ingredients

1 1/4 C Cassava Flour
1/4 C Tapioca Starch
1/4 C Butter
4 oz Cream Cheese
1 1/2 C Sugar + 1/2 C Set Aside
1/3 C Sunflower Oil
1 Egg, Large
1/2 TSP Baking Powder
1/2 TSP Guar Gum
1 TSP Salt
1 1/2 TSP Vanilla
1 TBS Milk of Choice

Chewy Sugar Cookies
Gluten, Tree Nut, Rice and Corn Free (Contains Dairy).

1. Preheat the oven to 350 degrees.

2. In the bowl of a stand mixer combine the butter, cream cheese, sugar and oil until combined and the mixture is smooth.

3. Add the egg, salt, guar gum and vanilla and combine until smooth.

4. Add the flours starting with the tapioca and then the cassava and mix until the dough forms. It will start to slightly ball but the mixture will still be soft.

5. Make balls about 1 TBS in size. Roll each ball in the reserved sugar and place on a baking sheet lined with parchment paper.

6. Continue until the pan is full leaving about 2 inches between each cookie. Slightly push down each cookie about 1/2 way down.

7. Bake the cookies at for about 12-15 minutes until the cookies start to become slightly golden on the bottoms and edges.

8. Allow to cool 5 minutes on the pan before transferring to a cooling rack to completely cool and enjoy!

Yield 24 Cookies

Coconut Flour Vanilla Cake

Gluten, Rice and Corn Free. (Diary Free Options, Contains Coconut).

Ingredients

8 Eggs, Large
1 C Sugar
1/2 C Oil
1/2 C Butter, Softened
1/8 C Milk of Choice
1 TBS Vanilla
1 TSP Baking Soda
1 TSP Cream of Tartar
1 TBS Apple Cider Vinegar
1/2 TSP Salt
3/4 C Coconut Flour
1/4 C Tapioca Starch

1. Preheat the oven to 350 degrees.

2. In the bowl of a stand mixer combine the sugar and butter until combined. You can sub the butter for equal parts oil but it will not give the same flavor as it would if using the butter.

3. Add the eggs one at a time while the mixer is on low to combine.

4. Add the vanilla, baking soda, cream of tartar and mix until combined.

5. Add the tapioca starch and coconut flour until combined.

6. Add the milk and apple cider vinegar and mix until combined and the mixture starts to look soft.

7. Add the oil and whip the mixture on high for about 5 min.

8. Pour mixture into prepared baking pans in desired sizes. Or fill cupcake liners about 1/2 full.

9. Baking the cake for about 25-30 min until a knife inserted comes out clean with just a few crumbs and the top bounces back with touched and is slightly golden.. For cupcakes bake about 18-20 minutes. until the tops are slightly golden.

10. Allow the cakes to cool completely before frosting and eating.

Yield 1-8 inch Cakes
or
12 Cupcakes

Classic Vanilla Buttercream Frosting

Gluten, Tree Nut. Rice and Corn Free. (Dairy Free Options).

1. In the bowl of a stand mixer combine the butter or palm shortening (if you want it to be dairy free) and the powdered sugar. Whisk on medium until combined.

2. Add the salt and vanilla then whisk again.

3. Depending on the consistency you want your frosting to be add the milk of choice in 1 tablespoon increments until desired consistency is achieved. If it becomes to wet, just add in more powdered sugar 1 tablespoon at a time.

Ingredients

1 C Butter, Softened or 1 C Palm Shortening
4 C Powdered Sugar
1/4 TSP Salt
1 TBS Vanilla
2-4 TBS Heavy Whipping Cream or Milk of Choice

Note: Traditional powdered sugars can be made with corn starch. I buy the Wholesome bran because is made with tapioca starch instead of corn starch which ensures it is grain free.

The palm shortening can be used in place of the butter. It will not yield the same exact flavor or texture but it is still a good choice for those wanting a dairy free option.

Yield 4 Cups

Coconut Flour Chocolate Cake

Gluten, Rice and Corn Free. (Diary Free Options, Contains Coconut).

Ingredients

1 C Butter or Ghee Soft
1 3/4 C Sugar
10 Eggs, Large
1 1/2 C Coconut Flour, Sifted
1 TBS Vanilla
1 3/4 C Milk of Choice
1/2 Avocado Oil
1 TSP Salt
1 1/2 TSP Baking Soda
1 C Cocoa Powder

1. Preheat the oven to 350 degrees.

2. Combine the butter or ghee with the sugar into the bowl of an electric mixer and mix on medium-high speed until light and fluffy.

3. Add the eggs one at a time and mix until combine between each egg.

4. Add the vanilla, milk and mix until combined.

5. Add the salt, baking soda and cocoa powder and mix until combined.

6. Add the coconut flour and mix until combined. The mixture will be slightly grainy at this point.

7. Lastly add the avocado oil to the mixture and mix on high until the mixture takes on a mouse like texture and the grainy texture goes away. This will take about 5-10 minutes.

8. While the oil is being whipped, grease and line your desired cake pans.

9. Fill batter about 1/2 way in the pan as it will expand while baking.

10. Bake for 25-30 minutes until the cake bounces back when its touched and a knife inserted comes out slightly crumby.

11. Allow the cake to fully cool before you ice it with your favorite icing or top it with my Avocado Mouse for an additional treat.

Yield 3-8 inch Cakes
or
24 Cupcakes

Ingredients

8 Oz Semi-Sweet Chocolate + 2 oz Set Aside
2 TBS Butter or Ghee
2 Eggs, Large
3/4 C Sugar
1 TSP Vanilla
1/2 C Arrowroot Starch
1/8 TSP Baking Soda
1/4 TSP Salt

Chewy Double Chocolate Cookies
Gluten, Tree Nut, Rice and Corn Free. (Dairy Free Options).

1. Melt the chocolate and butter in a bowl.

2. Whisk the chocolate and butter mixture until combined. Add the eggs, sugar and vanilla to the mixture and whisk again.

3. Add the baking soda and arrowroot and whisk till combined.

4. Fold in the mini chocolate chips, cover and chill for about 30 minutes to an hour.

5. Preheat the oven to 350 degrees and line a baking sheet with parchment paper and set aside.

6. Once the dough has chilled spoon about 1 tablespoon worth of dough onto the prepared baking sheet. Leave about 3 inches between each cookie as they will spread slightly.

7. Bake the cookies in the oven for about 10-12 minutes, until the tops look like they are starting to crack. (Think brownie tops.)

8. Allow the cookies to cool on the pan at least 5 minutes before transferring them to a cooling rack to finish cooling.

9. Repeat with remaining dough.

10. Let them cool and enjoy!

Note: I use Enjoy Life brand.

Chilling the dough keeps them from spreading as much. The longer you chill the dough the less they expand.

I like to keep this dough in the fridge to stay chilled between baking each batch.

Yield 24 Cookies

Grain Free Vanilla Extract
Gluten, Tree Nut, Rice, Corn and Dairy Free

1. Split 4-5 vanilla beans without cutting the beans all the way in half.

2. In a 2-4 OZ brown glass bottle add 4-5 of the split vanilla beans into the bottle.

3. Top with the grain free vodka of your choice.

4. Close and store in a dark place for at least 6 weeks before using. Flavor will intensify as it ages.

5. As you use some of the vanilla up add more vodka to the bottle and let it sit some more.

4-5 Grade B Madagascar Bourbon Vanilla Beans
80 Proof Grain Free Vodka
2-4 Oz Brown Glass Bottles

Note: I use Ciroc plain grape vodka. hey are distilled from grapes. A lot of traditional vanilla extracts are made from grain alcohols and can cause some issues with those with intolerances.

Make as may bottles as you and even give them away as holiday presents throughout the year for your grain free baking friends and family!

Opaque bottles work best for this recipe.

I like to keep 2-3 on hand and as I use one I add more vodka and rotate the bottles that are being use to let them sit as needed.

Yield 1 2-4 OZ Bottle

Grain Free Table

Written By Sara Vaughn

www.GrainFreeTable.com

Dedication

This book is dedicated to my girls. Many days have been spent with them in the kitchen testing recipes until they said they were just perfect! I will always cherish our times in the kitchen and I look forward to many years worth to come and many more recipes yet to be created!

To my husband, thank you for your support and humor indulging me in all the *many, many* failed recipe attempts over the years. You have always been my biggest supporter and I will always be thankful for that.

Sara Vaughn

Why I Wrote This Book!

I have always been someone who loves to cook and bake. I remember getting some of my grandmother's old cookbooks and wanting to try out all of the recipes in them. This love for cooking and baking just kept growing over time. I have even talked about wanting to open a bakery with my husband when we were first married. However, with us being a military family, we do not exactly get the luxury of staying in one place long periods of time to do that. Of course that has never stopped me from figuring out our daughters crazy birthday cake ideas over the years. It also has never stopped my husband from requesting special treats for himself or various work functions over the years either.

After I was diagnosed with celiac disease a few years ago, my love for cooking and baking never went away. At first it was frustrating because I realized how much I could not do anymore. Let's be honest, most "gluten free" things do not taste the best in stores. So instead of giving up, I set out just like before and tried to make what my family knew and loved my new cooking reality.

If you have not noticed by now, *most* gluten free products and recipes are still made from grains, usually *rice* and *corn*. In fact a lot of the pre-made gluten free flour blends are just this combination. While these sorts of blends work for many people who are avoiding gluten in their diets, it does not work for everyone. I am a perfect example of that. A little after my initial diagnosis, I was told that I was cross reactive to those *gluten free* grains. I was a confused at first and asked the doctors, "Cross reactive, what's that?" It turns out there is a percentage of celiacs who have to avoid more than just the typical "gluten" containing grains, which are wheat, barley and rye. Their systems actually illicit a response just as it would if they were to ingest gluten.

The most common cross reactive foods are:

Whey	Millet	Coffee
Casein	Corn	Oats
Milk chocolate	Rice	Potato
Brewer's and Baker's yeast		

Thankfully I was not reactive to *all* of those but I was reactive to all the *grains*. Which then meant that I had to do another about face in the way that I was eating and cooking, *again*. This time around I had to figure out how to make my families favorites completely *grain free* for us all to be able to enjoy them again.

This book is the product me of trying to figure out how to cook all over again. How I learned to make those classical meals that we all know and love. You know those meals I am talking about, those comfort foods filled with grains and gluten that we all thought we could not have anymore? Well I figured them out for you!

All of my recipes are completely 100% GRAIN FREE. I do however use some dairy and coconut derived products. I have worked hard to make as many variations to allow for changes to recipes for those who cannot have those as well..

We all want our food to taste good, right? Even when our diets are not always something we *want* to do but something rather we *have* to do. So I truly hope you enjoy these recipes as much as my family and I do!

My Favorite Flours!

Most *gluten* and *grain* free recipes use a variation of different flours and a lot of them also use nut flours, traditionally almond four. That is not the case for this book. The most used flours in this book are cassava flour, arrowroot starch, tapioca starch and coconut flour. I do add in some potato starch for some things but it is not something that I use *all* the time.

Cassava Flour

Cassava flour is a grain and nut free flour derived from the yucca root. This flour is becoming more and more popular in gluten free cooking and baking. A lot of people use cassava almost as a 1:1 sub for traditional flour and it can be done for *some* recipes. However, I find that still using it mixed with other flours yields a greater variety of textures for different foods.

Arrowroot Starch

Many people confuse arrowroot starch for cassava, while they are derived from the same yucca plant, they are not the same and not used interchangeably. Arrowroot has much less structure to it than cassava flour does and it is that difference that it cannot be used in the same way. However, when combined with cassava it has a tendency to lighten foods that can be left more dense with just cassava flour by itself.

Tapioca Starch

Tapioca starch is similar to arrowroot and is often used the same and interchangeably when using to thicken different sauces and soups. However tapioca starch does not stabilize the same as arrowroot or cassava flour when used for baking. It tends to react differently therefore, I like to keep this one around for when I need it to lighten up a dish.

Coconut Flour

While this book does not contain recipes using ingredients such as almond flour like a lot of other gluten free recipes. I do include some coconut flour in a few recipes. Therefor, I have listed all of these recipes with the tree nut notification. The reason for this is because coconut flour is technically considered a nut flour because coconut is classified as a *tree nut* by the FDA. I do not personally have a reaction to coconut flour so it is something that I use from time to time. I do know several people who do have a reaction and I wanted to make sure it was clear if that was in the recipe.

Coconut flour can be tricky to work it if it's not something you are used to. It does not convert in an equal ratio to wheat flour. In fact very little coconut flour is required as opposed to other grain free flours but that also means that other ingredients working with it have to be altered as well. Don't worry I've figured that all out for you!

Table of Contents

Veggies

Breads

Sweets

Lightning Source UK Ltd.
Milton Keynes UK
UKRC020923081019
351188UK00009B/66